RELIGIONS
OF THE
WORLD

BUDDHISM

CHRISTIANITY

CONFUCIANISM

HINDUISM

ISLAM

JUDAISM

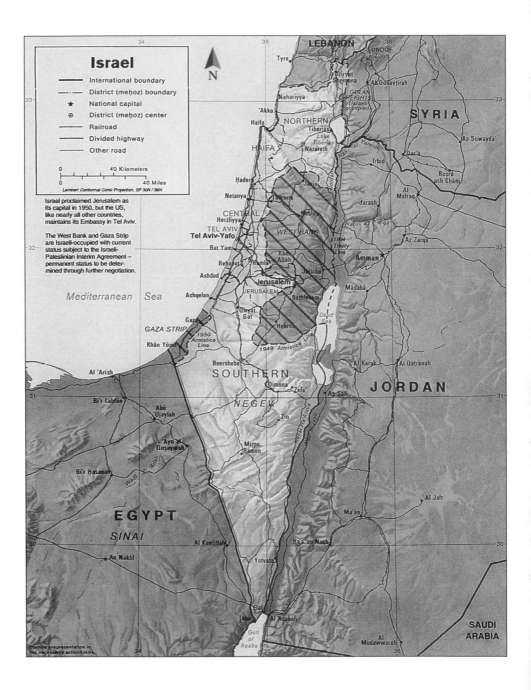

RELIGIONS
OF THE
WORLD

JUDAISM

Kenneth Atkinson
Assistant Professor of Religion,
The University of Northern Iowa
Department of Philosophy and Religion

Series Consulting Editor Ann Marie B. Bahr
Professor of Religious Studies,
South Dakota State University

Foreword by Martin E. Marty
Professor Emeritus,
University of Chicago Divinity School

CHELSEA HOUSE
PUBLISHERS
A Haights Cross Communications Company
Philadelphia

To my niece Kim Atkinson

FRONTIS Israel is a small nation on the banks of the Mediterranean Sea.
Ongoing tensions in the Middle East are the result of the fact that Israel, a
Jewish nation, is strongly opposed by the predominantly Muslim nations
that surround it, including Jordan, Syria, and Lebanon.

CHELSEA HOUSE PUBLISHERS

VP, NEW PRODUCT DEVELOPMENT Sally Cheney
DIRECTOR OF PRODUCTION Kim Shinners
CREATIVE MANAGER Takeshi Takahashi
MANUFACTURING MANAGER Diann Grasse

Staff for JUDAISM

EXECUTIVE EDITOR Lee Marcott
SENIOR EDITOR Tara Koellhoffer
PRODUCTION EDITOR Megan Emery
ASSISTANT PHOTO EDITOR Noelle Nardone
SERIES AND COVER DESIGNER Keith Trego
LAYOUT 21st Century Publishing and Communications, Inc.

A Haights Cross Communications ⌒ Company

www.chelseahouse.com

First Printing

9 8 7 6 5 4 3 2 1

Library of Congress Cataloging-in-Publication Data

Atkinson, Kenneth, 1960–
    Judaism/Kenneth Atkinson.
        p. cm.—(Religions of the world)
    Includes bibliographical references and index.
        ISBN 0-7910-7860-4   0-7910-8009-9
    1. Judaism. [1. Judaism.] I. Title. II. Series.
BM45.A85 2004
296—dc22

                                                          2003023921

CONTENTS

Foreword

O n this very day, like all other days, hundreds of millions of people around the world will turn to religion for various purposes.

On the one hand, there are purposes that believers in any or all faiths, as well as unbelievers, might regard as positive and benign. People turn to religion or, better, to their own particular faith, for the experience of healing and to inspire acts of peacemaking. They want to make sense of a world that can all too easily overwhelm them because it so often seems to be meaningless and even absurd. Religion then provides them with beauty, inspires their souls, and impels them to engage in acts of justice and mercy.

To be informed citizens of our world, readers have good reason to learn about these features of religions that mean so much to so many. Those who study the faiths do not have to agree with any of them and could not agree with all of them, different as they are. But they need basic knowledge of religions to understand other people and to work out strategies for living with them.

On the other hand—and religions always have an "other hand"—believers in any of the faiths, and even unbelievers who are against all of them, will find their fellow humans turning to their religions for purposes that seem to contradict all those positive features. Just as religious people can heal and be healed, they can also kill or be killed in the name of faith. So it has been through history.

This killing can be literal: Most armed conflicts and much terrorism today are inspired by the stories, commands, and promises that come along with various faiths. People can and do read and act upon scriptures that can breed prejudice and that lead them to reject other beliefs and believers. Or the killing can be figurative, which means that faiths can be deadening to the spirit. In the name of faith, many people are repressed, oppressed, sometimes victimized and abused.

If religion can be dangerous and if it may then come with "Handle with Care" labels, people who care for their own security, who want to lessen tensions and inspire concord, have to equip themselves by learning something about the scriptures and stories of their own and other faiths. And if they simply want to take delight in human varieties and imaginings, they will find plenty to please them in lively and reliable accounts of faiths.

A glance at television or at newspapers and magazines on almost any day will reveal stories that display one or both sides of religion. However, these stories usually have to share space with so many competing accounts, for example, of sports and entertainment or business and science, that writers and broadcasters can rarely provide background while writing headlines. Without such background, it is hard to make informed judgments.

The series RELIGIONS OF THE WORLD is designed to provide not only background but also rich illustrative material about the foreground, presenting the many features of faiths that are close at hand. Whoever reads all six volumes will find that these religions have some elements in common. Overall, one can deduce that their followers take certain things with ultimate seriousness: human dignity, devotion to the sacred, the impulse to live a moral life. Yet few people are inspired by religions in general. They draw strength from what they hold particularly. These particulars of each faith are not always contradictory to those of others, but they are different in important ways. It is simply a fact that believers are informed and inspired by stories told in separate and special ways.

A picture might make all this vivid: Reading about a religion, visiting a place of worship, or coming into the company of those who believe in and belong to a particular faith, is like entering a room. Religions are, in a sense, spiritual "furnished apartments." Their adherents have placed certain pictures on the wall and moved in with their own kind of furnishings, having developed their special ways of receiving or blocking out light from such places. Some of their figurative apartments are airy, and some stress strength and security.

Philosopher George Santayana once wrote that, just as we do not speak language, we speak particular languages, so we have religion not as a whole but as religions "in particular." The power of each living and healthy religion, he added, consists in "its special and surprising message and in the bias which that revelation gives to life." Each creates "another world to live in."

The volumes in this series are introductions to several spiritual furnished apartments, guides to the special and surprising messages of these large and complex communities of faith, or religions. These are not presented as a set of items in a cafeteria line down which samplers walk, tasting this, rejecting that, and moving on. They are not bids for window-shoppers or shoppers of any sort, though it may be that a person without faith might be drawn to one or another expression of the religions here described. The real intention of the series is to educate.

Education could be dull and drab. Picture a boring professor standing in front of a class and droning on about distant realities. The authors in this series, however, were chosen because they can bring readers up close to faiths and, sometimes better, to people of faith; not to religion but to people who are religious in particular ways.

As one walks the streets of a great metropolis, it is not easy and may not even be possible to deduce what are the faith-commitments of those one passes unless they wear a particular costume, some garb or symbol prescribed by their faith. There-fore, while passing them by, it is not likely that one can learn much about the dreams and hopes, the fears and intentions, of those around them.

These books, in effect, stop the procession of passersby and bid visitors to enter those sanctuaries where communities worship. Each book could serve as a guide to worship. Several years ago, a book called *How to Be a Perfect Stranger* offered brief counsel on how to feel and to be at home among worshipers from other traditions. This series recognizes that we are not strangers to each other only in sanctuaries. We carry over our attachments to conflicting faiths where we go to work or vote or serve in the military or have fun. These "carryovers" tend to come from the basic stories and messages of the several faiths.

The publishers have taken great pains to assign their work to authors of a particular sort. Had these been anti-religious or anti–the religion about which they write, they would have done a disservice. They would, in effect, have been blocking the figurative doors to the faiths or smashing the furniture in the sanctuaries. On the other hand, it would be wearying and distorting had the assignment gone to public relations agents, advertisers who felt called to claim "We're Number One!" concerning the faith about which they write.

Fair-mindedness and accuracy are the two main marks of these authors. In rather short compass, they reach a wide range of subjects, focusing on everything one needs to advance basic understanding. Their books are like mini-encyclopedias, full of information. They introduce the holidays that draw some neighbors to be absent from work or school for a day or a season. They include galleries of notable figures in each faith-community.

Since most religions in the course of history develop different ways in the many diverse places where they thrive, or because they attract intelligent, strong-willed leaders and writers, they come up with different emphases. They divide and split off into numberless smaller groups: Protestant and Catholic and Orthodox Christians, Shiite and Sunni Muslims, Orthodox and Reform Jews, and many kinds of Buddhists and Hindus. The writers in this series do justice to these variations, providing a kind of map without which one will get lost in the effort to understand.

Some years ago, a rabbi friend, Samuel Sandmel, wrote a book about his faith called *The Enjoyment of Scriptures*. What an astonishing concept, some might think: After all, religious scriptures deal with desperately urgent, life-and-death-and-eternity issues. They have to be grim and those who read them likewise. Not so. Sandmel knew what the authors of this series also know and impart: that the journeys of faith and the encounter with the religions of others include pleasing and challenging surprises. I picture many a reader coming across something on these pages that at first looks obscure or forbidding, but then, after a slightly longer look, makes sense and inspires an "aha!" There are many occasions for "aha-ing!" in these books. One can also wager that many a reader will come away from the encounters thinking, "I never knew that!" or "I never thought of that before." And they will be more ready than they had been to meet strangers of other faiths in a world that so many faiths *have* to share, or that they *get* to share.

Martin E. Marty, Professor Emeritus
The University of Chicago

Preface

The majority of people, both in the United States and around the world, consider religion to be an important part of their lives. Beyond its significance in individual lives, religion also plays an important role in war and peace, politics, social policy, ethics, and cultural expression. Yet few people feel well-prepared to carry on a conversation about religion with friends, colleagues, or their congressional delegation. The amount of knowledge people have about their own faith varies, but very few can lay claim to a solid understanding of a religion other than their own. As the world is drawn closer together by modern communications, and the religions of the world jostle each other in religiously plural societies, the lack of our ability to dialogue about this aspect of our lives results in intercultural conflict rather than cooperation. It means that individuals of different religious persuasions will either fight about their faiths or avoid the topic of religion altogether. Neither of these responses aids in the building of healthy, religiously plural societies. This gap in our knowledge is therefore significant, and grows increasingly more significant as religion plays a larger role in national and international politics.

The authors and editors of this series are dedicated to the task of helping to prepare present and future decision-makers to deal with religious pluralism in a healthy way. The objective scholarship found in these volumes will blunt the persuasive power of popular misinformation. The time is short, however. Even now, nations are dividing along religious lines, and "neutral" states as well as partisan religious organizations are precariously, if not always intentionally, tipping delicate balances of power in favor of one religious group or another with doles of aid and support for certain policies or political leaders. Intervention in the affairs of other nations is always a risky business, but doing it without understanding of the religious sensitivities of the populace dramatically increases the chances that even well-intentioned intervention will be perceived as political coercion or cultural invasion. With such signs of ignorance already manifest, the day of reckoning for educational policies that ignore the study of the world's religions cannot be far off.

This series is designed to bring religious studies scholarship to the leaders of today and tomorrow. It aims to answer the questions that students, educators, policymakers, parents, and citizens might have about the new religious milieu in which we find ourselves. For example, a person hearing about a religion that is foreign to him or her might want answers to questions like these:

- How many people believe in this religion? What is its geographic distribution? When, where, and how did it originate?

- What are its beliefs and teachings? How do believers worship or otherwise practice their faith?

- What are the primary means of social reinforcement? How do believers educate their youth? What are their most important communal celebrations?

- What are the cultural expressions of this religion? Has it inspired certain styles of art, architecture, literature, or music? Conversely, does it avoid art, literature, or music for religious reasons? Is it associated with elements of popular culture?

- How do the people who belong to this religion remember the past? What have been the most significant moments in their history?

- What are the most salient features of this religion today? What is likely to be its future?

We have attempted to provide as broad coverage as possible of the various religious forces currently shaping the planet. Judaism, Christianity, Islam, Hinduism, Buddhism, Confucianism, Taoism, Sikhism, and Shinto have each been allocated an entire volume. In recognition of the fact that many smaller ancient and new traditions also exercise global influence, we present coverage of some of these in two additional volumes titled "Tribal Religions" and "New Religions." Each volume in the series discusses demographics and geography, founder or foundational period, scriptures, worldview, worship or practice, growing up in the religion, cultural expressions, calendar and holidays, history, and the religion in the world today.

The books in this series are written by scholars. Their approach to their subject matter is neutral and objective. They are not trying to convert readers to the religion they are describing. Most scholars, however, value the religion they have chosen to study, so you can expect the general tone of these books to be appreciative rather than critical.

Religious studies scholars are experts in their field, but they are not critics in the same sense in which one might be an art, film, or literary critic. Religious studies scholars feel obligated to describe a tradition faithfully and accurately, and to interpret it in a way that will allow nonbelievers as well as believers to grasp its essential structure, but they do not feel compelled to pass judgment on it. Their goal is to increase knowledge and understanding.

Academic writing has a reputation for being dry and uninspiring. If so, religious studies scholarship is an exception. Scholars of religion have the happy task of describing the words and deeds of some of the world's most amazing people: founders, prophets, sages, saints, martyrs, and bodhisattvas.

The power of religion moves us. Today, as in centuries past, people thrill to the ethical vision of Confucianism, or the dancing beauty of Hinduism's images of the divine. They are challenged by the one, holy God of the Jews, and comforted by the saving promise of Christianity. They are inspired by the stark purity of

Islam, by the resilience of tribal religions, by the energy and innovation of the new religions. The religions have retained such a strong hold on so many people's lives over such a long period of time largely because they are unforgettable.

Religious ideas, institutions, and professions are among the oldest in humanity's history. They have outlasted the world's great empires. Their authority and influence have endured far beyond that of Earth's greatest philosophers, military leaders, social engineers, or politicians. It is this that makes them so attractive to those who seek power and influence, whether such people intend to use their power and influence for good or evil. Unfortunately, in the hands of the wrong person, religious ideas might as easily be responsible for the destruction of the world as for its salvation. All that stands between us and that outcome is the knowledge of the general populace. In this as in any other field, people must be able to critically assess what they are being told.

The authors and editors of this series hope that all who seek to wield the tremendous powers of religion will do so with unselfish and noble intent. Knowing how unlikely it is that that will always be the case, we seek to provide the basic knowledge necessary to critically assess the degree to which contemporary religious claims are congruent with the history, scriptures, and genius of the traditions they are supposed to represent.

1

Introduction

This is a turning point in our history.
During more than 2,000 years of exile,
generations of Jews fought and struggled
to get back the homeland we lost.
Now, after the founding of the state,
our main task is to secure, reestablish,
and develop the homeland we got back.

—Former Israeli Prime Minister
Benjamin Netanyahu,
January 10, 1996

What is Judaism? Who is a Jew? Is Judaism a religion, a nationality, or a culture? These may sound like simple questions, but they are actually quite difficult to answer. Judaism is one of the world's oldest religions. It began in the Bronze Age (approximately 2000–1500 B.C.), when a man named Abraham claimed he was called by God to leave his ancestral homeland in modern-day Iraq and move to a new country. Later, people like Moses and David added new practices and beliefs to Judaism.

Judaism continued to grow and go through modifications from the biblical period up to the present. It has undergone many other changes over the past 4,000 years, as Jews have moved away from their ancestral homeland in the Middle East. Judaism is now practiced all over the world, and there are many different forms: Some are conservative, while others are liberal. There is no single definition or criteria to determine who is a Jew. Jews still disagree over who should be considered a Jew and what is the essence of Judaism.

Despite Judaism's diversity, all of its forms revere the Jewish Scriptures and believe in one God. Because of its emphasis on Scripture, Judaism is referred to as a "religion of the book." Judaism, moreover, is unique among the world's religions because both Christianity and Islam trace their heritage to Judaism. Both of these faiths accept the Jewish Scriptures, as well as many Jewish teachings and customs. For this reason, it is impossible to fully understand Christianity and Islam without first learning about Judaism.

SIZE AND DISTRIBUTION

In 1948, Israel, an officially Jewish nation, was founded. The majority of Jews live outside the land of Israel. Today, there are approximately 12.8 million Jews scattered around the world. This number is somewhat deceptive, however. It should be considerably larger. Before World War II began in 1939, there were approximately 15.3 million Jews in the world. Nearly 9.5 million lived in Europe. Approximately

6 million Jews were murdered during the Holocaust, the genocidal event in which Nazi Germany attempted to eliminate all Jews. By 1950, the Jewish population of Europe had been reduced to about 3.5 million. Since the tragic events of the Holocaust, the Jewish population has increased throughout Europe, but has never fully recovered. In some areas of Europe, entire Jewish communities were exterminated. Many of these towns and villages were never resettled, and in some regions of Eastern Europe, Jewish life ceased entirely after the Holocaust.

With the creation of the modern nation of Israel in 1948, many Jews left Europe to escape further persecution. Today, Israel has the second largest Jewish community in the world, numbering nearly 5 million. Some 7.8 million Jews live elsewhere. The United States has the largest Jewish population, with approximately 6 million. This means that there are very few Jews in other countries. Since the end of World War II, the United States and Israel have replaced Europe as the centers of contemporary Judaism. Although many Jews in modern times have moved to either Israel or the United States, there are still Jewish communities scattered in more than one hundred countries around the world. Approximately half a million Jews live in Asia. The North African Jewish population has decreased since 1948 because of immigration to Israel, Europe, and the United States. In Morocco, for example, the Jewish community has shrunk from 200,000 to under 20,000. Some thirty countries, including Afghanistan and Bahrain, now contain fewer than a hundred Jews.

WHO IS A JEW?

Some Jews believe that Judaism is more than a religion: They consider Judaism a culture, a lifestyle, or a nationality. Therefore, Jews are people who practice the religion of Judaism, or who recognize themselves as ethnically or culturally Jewish. Judaism is different from Christianity and Islam, because identifying oneself as Jewish does not depend upon accepting particular beliefs or religious customs.

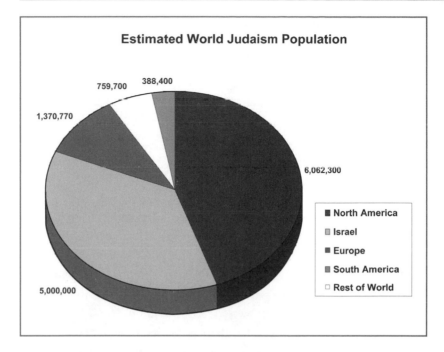

Estimated World Judaism Population

759,700   388,400

1,370,770

6,062,300

- North America
- Israel
- Europe
- South America
- Rest of World

5,000,000

This pie chart, reproduced based on information from the World Jewish Congress, provides estimates of the world's Jewish population in the early years of the twenty-first century, broken down by the location where the people live. Although Israel boasts a huge population of Jews—5 million—North America actually is home to more Jewish people—largely because the United States has long been a popular destination for Jewish immigrants.

Because Judaism is such an ancient religion, it is very diverse. It has constantly adapted in response to changing historical circumstances. Because Jews have been persecuted throughout history, it has often been dangerous for people to be identified publicly as Jews. Since Jews have not until recently created their own country, there was no need in the past for them to conduct a census. Today, it is difficult to determine the worldwide Jewish population, since there is no single official body whose definition of Judaism all Jews would recognize. For this reason, all the facts and figures concerning Judaism's size and geographical distribution can only be approximate. Over time, many Jews have adopted the surrounding secular culture, and no longer identify themselves as practicing, or religious, Jews. In spite of this, many secular Jews still consider themselves Jewish. Because they are not affiliated with a synagogue, the Jewish place of worship, however, their numbers are difficult to calculate.

In the past, most Jews considered birth to be the major factor that determined whether a person is Jewish. Traditionally, a person was considered Jewish if he or she had a Jewish mother. This system makes it easy to determine who is a Jew, since the identity of a person's mother is never in doubt. Some contemporary forms of Judaism, such as the Orthodox movement, still believe that the religion of one's mother decides whether a person is Jewish. On the other hand, the modern Jewish movement known as Reform Judaism also recognizes children born of Jewish fathers as Jewish.

Although Judaism has traditionally been determined by birth, Gentiles, or non-Jews, can convert to Judaism. Converts must believe in one God and accept the basic teachings of Judaism found in the Jewish Scriptures and other sacred books. In Judaism, males must be circumcised eight days after birth. This tradition goes back to Abraham, who was told by God that all males must be circumcised as a sign of God's covenant with the Jewish people. Adult males who convert are still circumcised today, to show that they belong to the religion of Judaism.

Judaism has experienced many forced displacements of its people, and much persecution by members of other religions throughout its history. For centuries, few people converted to Judaism because the Christian Church banned it and persecuted Jews. In the Islamic world, Jews generally experienced better conditions than Jews in Europe did. For many centuries, Muslims were more tolerant of Jews than Christians were. Jews in regions such as Spain and the Middle East prospered under Islamic rule. Throughout most of Europe, on the other hand, the persecution of Jews, called anti-Semitism, gradually led to the separation of Jews from their Gentile neighbors. Jews were frequently restricted to certain occupations and forced to live in segregated, crowded portions of cities called ghettos. Judaism, however, has always taught that one did not have to be Jewish to achieve spiritual salvation; Gentiles, too, could be saved. Gentiles who converted to Judaism risked persecution, and Jews often tried to dissuade them from doing so because conversion is considered unnecessary for salvation.

IS JUDAISM A NATIONALITY OR A LIFESTYLE?

The nation of Israel, in the Middle East, is the world's only Jewish state. It was created in 1948 after World War II and the Holocaust. In order to escape further persecution, many Jews moved to the region formerly known as Palestine and established the modern nation of Israel. The majority of people who live in Israel are Jews, and the official calendar is Jewish. Jewish religious holidays, and not Christian celebrations such as Christmas, are recognized. Jewish customs and practices are largely taken for granted. The Jews in Israel have revived Hebrew, the language of the Jewish Scriptures, as a spoken language.

Because Israel was created as a Jewish homeland, it continues to welcome Jews from around the world. The Israeli government grants citizenship to any person with a Jewish mother, or anyone who has converted to Judaism. Sometimes this law has been extended to include the non-Jewish family members of Jews. Today, some Israeli citizens are questioning the traditional definition of Judaism, and want to expand it to include people with Jewish fathers. Although Israel is important to contemporary Judaism, the majority of the world's Jews do not live there. As a result, it would be incorrect to view Judaism as a national identity.

Judaism is considered by some to be a lifestyle. Judaism traditionally requires its adherents to follow certain food restrictions and religious practices that separate Jews from Gentiles. Some Jews are strict in their observance of the ancient Jewish laws, and avoid food such as pork. Jews worship on the

Sabbath, which, according to the Jewish calendar, begins on Friday evening and ends on Saturday evening. (Christians generally consider Sunday the Sabbath, instead of Saturday.) Despite differing practices that have historically separated Jews from Gentiles, Judaism has always tolerated diversity and recognizes that there are many different ways to be Jewish. Because many Jews no longer follow the traditional Jewish laws, however, it is inaccurate to consider the entire religion of Judaism a lifestyle.

CULTURAL DIVISIONS OF JUDAISM

Because Judaism is such an ancient faith, it has become more than a religion. Many Jews consider Judaism a culture. As Judaism expanded around the world, it gradually adopted many new cultural practices. These traditions, for many Jews today, are just as important as the different ways to observe Judaism. Many Jews, regardless of the way they practice Judaism, incorporate elements from one of the two dominant Jewish cultures: Sephardim and Ashkenazim.

During the centuries of Muslim rule, the Jewish community in Spain became quite large. Muslim power in Europe was at its height in the 700s, but Muslims held on to Spain for centuries after that. Jews in Spain developed many common customs, as well as a language called Ladino, which combined Hebrew and Spanish. Jews in other nations under Muslim rule, such as Morocco, Greece, Egypt, and other countries surrounding the Mediterranean Sea, developed a similar culture. Jews who can trace their heritage to these regions are known as Sephardic Jews, or Sephardim. There is still a large Sephardic community in Morocco. Today, more than half the Jews in Israel are of Sephardic ancestry. They speak Hebrew with a particular accent and they worship differently from Jews of European heritage.

Jews from Central Europe, who developed very different cultural practices and traditions from those of the Jews in the Middle East, became known as Ashkenazi Jews. The

Ashkenazim generally lived in Poland, Lithuania, Germany, Hungary, and other Eastern European countries. Their common language is Yiddish, which is a medieval form of German that includes many Hebrew words. The distinctive culture of Ashkenazi Jews in Europe largely ended with the Holocaust. Today, Jews of Ashkenazi heritage usually live in the United States, Canada, and Israel.

The Ashkenazim and Sephardim recognize each other as Jewish, though they have developed different customs and forms of worship. Sephardic and Ashkenazi Jews adopted many distinct cultural practices from their ancestral homelands. They normally spoke their traditional languages and wore certain styles of dress. Some still maintain these cultural practices. The Sephardim have been more open than the Ashkenazim to secular culture. This is likely because they originated in countries that had diverse populations and were more tolerant of Judaism.

Although these two Jewish communities are the largest, there are others. The Jews of Ethiopia practice a very unusual type of Judaism. They claim to be descendants of the biblical King Solomon and the Queen of Sheba. They accept only the first five books of the Jewish Scriptures, and they practice a more ancient form of Judaism. Many have recently migrated to Israel. Jews are also found throughout the Middle East and in several Asian countries. Little is known about some of these smaller Jewish communities, since they have largely lived in isolation from the outside world for centuries.

The Samaritans are a religious group that is closely related to Judaism. Although the Samaritan religion began as a form of Judaism, over time it has come to be regarded as a separate faith. The word *Samaritan* refers to a person who believes that Mount Gerizim, located north of Jerusalem—and not Jerusalem itself—was chosen by God as the central place of worship. This faith was later given the name "Samaritan" after the region of Samaria in central Israel where Mount Gerizim is found.

There is still a debate concerning the exact origins of the Samaritans. Many scholars believe that the Samaritans can be traced back to a story in 2 Kings 17, in which the Assyrians, after deporting some Jews from Samaria, settled pagans in the region. The remaining Jews who were not deported intermarried with some of these pagans and adopted foreign religious practices. Because of their intermarriage with pagans, many Jews no longer considered them to be Jewish. Centuries later, the Jews in the southern kingdom were deported to modern-day Iraq by the Babylonians. When they were allowed to return to Jerusalem, they did not allow the Samaritans to participate in rebuilding the Jerusalem Temple because they considered them impure. The Samaritans, however, have a different version of their history. They believe that their ancestors were the descendants of Israelites from the Northern Kingdom who were not deported by the Assyrians.

The beliefs of the Samaritans differ from Judaism in a number of ways. In the past, the Samaritans had their own temple on Mount Gerizim, which they believed was the true holy place selected by God. Mount Gerizim, although lacking a temple today, is still an important religious pilgrimage site for the Samaritans.

The Samaritans follow a slightly different version of the Pentateuch, the first five books of the Bible. In their version, Mount Gerizim is mentioned as the sacred place. Most Jews believe that the Samaritans have added these references to Mount Gerizim to the original text of the Jewish Scriptures. Some scholars believe that the Samaritans and their version of the Bible date back to the second century B.C. and that this religion is not as old as was once thought.

Like Jews, the Samaritans revere Moses. The Samaritans also expect a *Taheb*, a Messiah, to appear at the end of days. By the time of Jesus, the Samaritans and Jews did not generally associate with one another. Jesus frequently refers to Samaritans in the New Testament and even once told a story about a "Good Samaritan" who was a righteous person (Book of Luke 10; see also John 4). There is still a small Samaritan community in Israel today. The majority of Jewish rabbis do not consider them Jews.

The Karaites are another group that, like the Samaritans, follows a slightly different text of the Jewish Scriptures. Unlike the Samaritans, the Karaites *are* regarded as Jews. Some Jews, however, believe that they practice a corrupt version of the faith. The Karaites reject the Oral Torah, which means they do not follow the traditions and teachings of the Talmud. The founder of Karaism was a man named Anan ben David, a prominent Jewish scholar in Babylon during the eighth century A.D. He opposed the rabbinical movement and its emphasis on the Talmud.

The Karaite religion at one time was very prominent and had large communities throughout Europe and the Middle East. During the Holocaust, the Karaites were largely spared persecution because the Nazis did not consider them Jews. Most Karaites today live in Israel, where they number some thirty thousand.

Because they follow only the teachings of the Jewish Scriptures, their religious practices and customs differ from those of most Jews. For example, they follow much less restrictive dietary regulations than the more conservative branches of Judaism do. Unlike other Jews, Karaites require worshipers to remove their shoes before entering the synagogue. The Karaites even believe that the Muslims later adopted this custom from them.

MAIN SUBDIVISIONS OF JUDAISM

There are many answers to the question of who is a Jew. Some Jews regard Judaism as a culture or nationality, while others consider it a lifestyle. The majority of Jews emphasize observance when they define Judaism. A person must *do* something to be Jewish. In the past, most Jews were traditional and practiced Judaism the way their ancestors had done for centuries. In the modern period, beginning around the eighteenth century in Germany, Judaism has increasingly adapted to the changing world by adjusting its beliefs. Today, there are four major sub-divisions of Judaism: Orthodox, Conservative, Reform, and Reconstructionist. Because there is also a large assimilated Jewish community, there are also other new forms of Judaism still emerging that are much less religious than the conventional four subdivisions.

ORTHODOX JUDAISM

Orthodox Judaism is the traditional form of Judaism. Although Orthodox Judaism has changed over time to adapt to historical events and new circumstances, it has always remained firmly rooted in tradition. It attempts to follow many of the ancient laws that were preserved in written form in the Jewish Scriptures, as well as other laws that were passed down orally through successive generations of Jewish religious leaders called *rabbis*. Orthodox Jews observe the biblical kosher laws that prohibit certain foods, including pork. They also rest on the Sabbath, the seventh day of the week, as commanded in the Jewish Scriptures. Hebrew, the language of the Jewish Scriptures, is still used in worship. Women in Orthodox Judaism must cover their heads and sit apart from men during worship. Men are required to keep their heads covered at all times to remind them that God is above everything. Orthodox Jewish men traditionally leave their beards and the hair in front of their ears uncut, in accordance with the Jewish Scriptures (Leviticus 19:27).

Until the Holocaust, Yiddish was widely spoken by Orthodox Jews throughout Europe. Yiddish, which became the dominant language of daily life in many regions, is a mixture of German and Hebrew, written in the Hebrew alphabet. Many Orthodox Jewish communities still use Yiddish in daily life, and speak Hebrew during worship services. Such linguistic differences have further divided Orthodox Jews from their Gentile neighbors, who do not speak Yiddish or Hebrew. Orthodox Judaism was largely destroyed in Europe as a result of the Holocaust. In Israel, the Orthodox comprise approximately one-tenth of the population. Despite their small numbers, Orthodox Jews have become more active in Israeli politics in recent decades. They now wield considerable political influence in their efforts to promote Orthodox causes, such as education and ensuring that civil laws do not violate the tenets of their faith.

During the centuries when Christians in Europe persecuted Jews, many Orthodox communities developed their own distinctive culture. In many regions, for example, Yiddish became the dominant language of daily life. Because Orthodox Jews follow strict dietary laws, they have traditionally lived apart from other people. There are still communities, such as the "ultraorthodox," whose members seek to separate themselves from Gentiles.

The ultraorthodox practice the strictest interpretation of Judaism. They are more conservative than most Orthodox Jews. Many ultraorthodox dress in black coats and hats, as their ancestors did in Central Europe during the nineteenth century, the period when the movement first developed.

In recent decades, some Orthodox Jews have embraced selected aspects of modernity. Many no longer seek to live apart from Gentiles, and have tried to integrate into modern society. Without abandoning their religious customs and beliefs, many have sought social and political positions. Some Orthodox Jews allow their children to attend secular schools. Others, however, prefer to send their children to separate schools run by the Orthodox Jewish community that combine education with religious instruction.

CONSERVATIVE JUDAISM

Conservative Judaism is the largest branch of Judaism in the United States. This subdivision traces its origin to Jews in the nineteenth century who thought that the liberal Reform movement had become too extreme. Conservative Judaism seeks to strike a balance between the strict beliefs of Orthodox Jews and the liberal practices of Reform Jews. Though it is firmly rooted in the traditions of Orthodox Judaism, Conservative Judaism rejects many Orthodox Jewish traditions in favor of the scientific study of the Bible and other Jewish texts. Conservative Judaism believes that Judaism has always changed, and that Jews have adapted their laws and beliefs in order to make them relevant to the times. Like their ancestors, Conservative Jews believe that they must adapt Judaism to the modern world while maintaining continuity with past customs and traditions.

Many Conservative Jews follow the regulations about kosher food and Sabbath observance that are found in the Jewish Scriptures and in a Jewish book known as the Talmud. Conservative Judaism, for example, has retained the traditional Saturday morning worship, and men cover their heads during religious services. Although Conservative Judaism is open to change, it emphasizes that study and discussion must precede any innovation. Conservative Judaism originally rejected Zionism, the movement to create a Jewish homeland in Israel, as well as the ordination of women rabbis. After much discussion and reflection, it later reversed itself and now accepts the existence of the state of Israel and women rabbis. These remain controversial topics for many Jews, because some believe that only God can re-create the ancestral Jewish nation. Conservative Judaism's changes regarding these issues demonstrate its willingness to reconsider its beliefs.

The Jewish Theological Seminary of America, in New York City, has emerged as the major voice of Conservative Judaism in the United States. Students at this Jewish university study the traditional Jewish texts and Scriptures from a historical-critical point of view, viewing them as writings that have grown over time and were produced by humans. This acceptance of new methods of studying the Bible is one of the major features that distinguish Conservative Judaism from Orthodox Judaism.

REFORM JUDAISM
The name "Orthodox Judaism" was not used until the liberal movement known as Reform Judaism emerged in the early to mid-1800s. Once there was a new liberal movement, the more

traditional form of Judaism needed a name to distinguish it from its less observant counterpart. Similarly, Conservative Judaism also emerged as a distinct subdivision of Judaism after the creation of Reform Judaism. It adopted the name "Conservative" to distinguish itself from both Orthodox and Reform Judaism.

Reform Judaism began in nineteenth-century Germany as an attempt to modernize Judaism. The early founders of Reform Judaism wanted to merge the Jewish faith with modern German culture. Many Jews wanted to remain Jewish, but wished to be identified first as citizens of Germany, and then as Jews. They were open to new scientific advances, such as the historical-critical study of religions texts and a more secular and historical outlook regarding the development of civilization, and rejected many of their ancestral traditions.

The Reform movement shortened the traditional Sabbath service and allowed Jews to use their own everyday language, rather than Hebrew, in worship. Men and women sit together in the synagogue as they worship with uncovered heads. Some Reform congregations use organs and choirs, and services are usually held on Friday night. The Reform movement abandoned the traditional form of dress still worn by many Orthodox Jews. Reform Jews are not required to adhere to kosher food restrictions or follow the laws in the ancient traditions recorded in the Talmud. Reform Judaism also ordains women as rabbis. This form of Judaism is especially popular in the United States and Europe.

RECONSTRUCTIONIST JUDAISM

Reconstructionist Judaism grew out of Conservative Judaism. It is the newest and smallest branch of Judaism. An American Conservative Jewish rabbi named Mordecai M. Kaplan (1881–1983), who taught at the Jewish Theological Seminary of America, founded Reconstructionist Judaism. He considered Judaism both a culture and a religion. Kaplan taught that Judaism was an evolving religious civilization. In his view, Jews needed to study the entire history of Jewish culture in order to know how to be Jewish, and he believed that Judaism periodically had to be updated.

Reconstructionist Judaism does not interpret the Bible and traditional Jewish texts literally. Kaplan also departed from traditional Judaism in a dramatic way when he denied that God had chosen the Jewish people as the line of descent that would come to occupy Israel and through which the Messiah would come. Kaplan taught that the Jewish people had always tried of their own accord to become the people of God. He also interpreted many elements of traditional Jewish belief, such as angels and the Messiah, as symbols, rather than as actual physical beings. Women may become rabbis in Reconstructionist Judaism.

OTHER FORMS OF JUDAISM

There are a few other forms of Judaism, such as Ethiopian Judaism, that cannot easily be classified within one of the four major subdivisions of Judaism. There is also a Jewish form of fundamentalism that teaches a strict interpretation of traditional Jewish law and is openly hostile to Gentiles. Some of these fundamentalist groups, such as the United Association of Movements for the Holy Temple (UAMHT), have recently sought to remove Muslims from Jewish regions of Israel and Jerusalem. Some groups, including the Lifta Gang, even use terrorism to expel Muslims from Israel. In recent decades, many of these groups have moved to Israel to establish Jewish

THE FUTURE OF JUDAISM?

The birthrate of Jews in the Dispersion is too low and the attractions of assimilation are too great. Admittedly, Israel will remain in the hands of people who are descended from Jews, but increasingly some commentators believe that in future decades they too will intermarry with the surrounding nations and will perceive themselves as Israelis rather than as Jews.

From Dan Cohn-Sherbok, *Judaism*. Upper Saddle River, NJ: Prentice Hall, 1999, p. 110.

settlements in lands dominated by Muslims. They have come into conflict with both the Jewish authorities and the Muslims in Israel.

Many Jews are secular, or nonobservant. They do not openly practice Judaism, but nevertheless consider themselves Jews by birth or culture. This may sound strange, but it is also true of people of other religions, such as Christianity. In the United States, for example, many people identify themselves as Christians, even though they do not attend church services. Secular Jews identify with Judaism and may observe some Jewish holidays, although few regularly attend religious services. These Jews are difficult to identify or count, because many do not live in Jewish communities or openly refer to themselves as Jewish. It is even possible for people to be atheists and still be considered Jewish, if they identify with Judaism's history and ethical system.

JUDAISM'S CHANGING FACE

Even with a great deal of study, it is very difficult to find a single correct answer to questions about what Judaism is, who is a Jew, and whether Judaism is a religion, a nationality, or a culture. Judaism is one of the richest and most diverse religions in the world today. Jews agree to disagree over many of their faith's most basic teachings and practices. All Jews, however, are united in their belief that they are somehow connected with the ancient Jewish figures of the past.

2

Foundations

Now the Lord said to Abram,
"Go forth from your country,
And from your relatives
And from your father's house,
To the land which I will show you;
And I will make you a great nation. . . ."

—Genesis 12:1–2

Judaism is one the world's oldest religions. Because it has existed for thousands of years, Judaism emphasizes history. Story is central to the Jewish faith. Many contemporary Jewish rituals and ceremonies act out events from the past that are recorded in the Jewish Scriptures.

The history of Judaism is a long tale that begins in ancient Mesopotamia, which was located in present-day Iraq. Judaism has not a single founder, but many foundational figures, each of whom added something new to the faith. All Jews, despite their theological differences, believe that they are connected spiritually with the people whose stories are told in the Jewish Scriptures. Contemporary Judaism still looks to its ancient scriptural texts to determine modern practices. Judaism is essentially a story about God's past actions on behalf of the Jewish people. It is, therefore, necessary to understand Judaism's early history, as described in the Jewish Scriptures, in order to understand modern Judaism.

ABRAHAM

The ancient Jewish Scriptures contain stories about the creation of the world, the first humans, and humanity's early history. These stories are told to emphasize that there is one God, who is responsible for all creation. In ancient times, people commonly worshiped many gods. Many people of antiquity looked at the forces of nature around them and believed that they were alive. They worshiped nature, and offered sacrifices of animals and plants to appease the gods in an effort to control their environment. Some of these ancient deities were believed to be male, and others were female. The gods and goddesses of antiquity even married and fought with one another like humans do. This type of religion, in which there is the worship of more than one god, is called *polytheism*. Most polytheistic religions teach that there are different gods who are responsible for each nation or region.

Judaism actually begins with a man named Abraham, who is also a foundational figure for Christianity and Islam. All three of these religions believe that Abraham was called by God and was the first person to practice *monotheism*, which is the belief in a single God. Abraham and his male descendants are called the "patriarchs." Most scholars believe that Abraham lived sometime between 1900 and 1700 B.C. The stories about the patriarchs are found in Genesis, the first book of the Bible.

Abraham lived in a city called Ur of the Chaldeans, located in southern Iraq. He was born into a culture that was dominated by polytheism. Abraham belonged to a group of people referred to as "Semitic," or "Semites." This name does not refer exclusively to Jews; it includes other peoples from the countries of the ancient Middle East and North Africa. It was originally a regional and ethnic term, not a racial epithet. The Semites spoke a language that was a precursor of Hebrew, the primary language of the Jewish Scriptures.

According to the Bible, God told Abraham and his family to leave their home in Ur and go to a new land. God promised Abraham that his descendants would become a great nation. Abraham and his family left Ur and eventually reached the land of Canaan, a region that encompasses portions of the modern

THE JEWISH SCRIPTURES

Jews frequently refer to their Scriptures as the *Tanakh*. This word is actually an acronym. It was created when Jews took the first letter of the Hebrew name for each of the divisions of the Bible (*Torah*=Law; *Nevi'im*=Prophets; and *Kethuvim*=Writings) and inserted vowels to come up with the term *Tanakh*. Some Jews refer to the *Tanakh* as the Hebrew Scriptures or the Hebrew Bible, because the majority of these books are written in Hebrew. A few books of the Bible are actually written in Aramaic, a language that is related to Hebrew.

The religion of Christianity accepted the Tanakh. Christians later used *testament*, the Latin word for "covenant," as a name for the Tanakh and their own Scriptures. They began to call the Tanakh the "Old Testament" (old covenant), and their own Scriptures the "New Testament" (new covenant). Jews today usually refer to their Scriptures as the Tanakh since the names *Old Testament* and *New Testament* are actually Christian terms.

nations of Israel, Jordan, Palestine, and Syria. The Bible calls this entire territory "Israel," even though it is larger than the modern state of Israel. It is named after one of Abraham's descendants. The Romans called this region "Palestine." Contemporary Judaism prefers the term "Israel," because it is the name most frequently used in the Bible. The Jewish people were originally called Hebrews, and then Israelites. The Israelites later became known as Jews.

In exchange for their agreeing to leave their home, God promised to make Abraham and his family a great nation, and to bless the peoples of the earth through Abraham's descendants. This promise is known as the covenant. A covenant is a legally binding agreement or contract between two parties. The Jewish covenant is unique because it was entirely based on a belief in one God. This covenant did not include any laws or rules about how to be Jewish. In fact, the religion it helped found at this time was not even called "Judaism." Abraham's family and the community that practiced monotheism are frequently called "the Hebrews" in the early books of the Jewish Scriptures. Abraham is even called "Abraham the Hebrew." The word *Hebrew*, like *Semite*, is not a racial designation. It is simply used to refer to Abraham and his monotheistic community.

At first, Abraham's new religion was largely restricted to members of his family. Like the polytheists around him, Abraham worshipped God by sacrificing animals, a common practice in the ancient Middle East. At this point, there was nothing, other than the belief in only one God, to distinguish Abraham's religion from polytheism. Later, the Jews received a code of laws and regulations to follow, as well as additional promises to be part of the covenant. Because the covenant in the Jewish Scriptures grew over time, there are actually several foundational figures in Jewish history whose teachings and deeds continue to shape the religion even today. Traditional Jews, on the other hand, believe that the stories about Judaism's origins are completely factual.

The Jewish Scriptures contain many stories about Abraham's struggles to reach the new land. God eventually led him to the land called Canaan, named after its original inhabitants, the Canaanites. (Later, the land of Canaan became known as Israel.) The Canaanites, like other people of the day, practiced polytheism. Because Abraham was an outsider, he was not always welcomed by the Canaanites. As Abraham and his family grew more prosperous, the Canaanites became afraid of their power. Canaanites did not always feel comfortable with the fact that Abraham's community did not recognize the existence of their gods.

When a famine struck the Middle East, Abraham and his family had to leave Canaan for Egypt in order to find food. Despite his troubles, the Scriptures insist that Abraham was always blessed. According to Judaism, the covenant with God did not guarantee Abraham and his people material prosperity or happiness; the blessing of the covenant was simply a relationship with God. Even though Abraham had to leave Canaan, he knew that he would someday return, because God had promised the land to his descendants.

Abraham eventually did return to the land of Canaan. God then appeared to Abraham and ordered him to circumcise all males, as a sign of the covenant. Circumcision was a very ancient religious custom that was practiced by groups such as the Egyptians. God told Abraham that all future male children must be circumcised eight days after birth. Circumcision became a sign of faith in the one God, and the covenant. People who wanted to practice this religion had to believe in the one God and, if male, undergo circumcision. These two requirements remain Jewish traditions to the present day.

Abraham and his wife, Sarah, grew very old. Because they had no children and did not own any land, it looked as though God were not going to fulfill the covenant. Sarah began to doubt that they would be able to have any children together to inherit their property. So, Sarah asked Abraham, who was then eighty-six years old, to have children for her, through their female Egyptian slave, Hagar. Abraham agreed, and had a child with Hagar, a boy named Ishmael. Over time, Sarah became jealous of Hagar and her son. She convinced Abraham to send Hagar and Ishmael away into the desert. God, however, sent an angel to protect Hagar and Ishmael. Today, the religion of Islam traces its heritage through Abraham's son Ishmael.

God told Abraham that the covenant would yet be fulfilled and that he would have a child with Sarah. Abraham and Sarah eventually had a son, named Isaac. According to the Jewish Scriptures, Abraham was one hundred years old when Isaac was born. Now, the land was the only part of the covenant that had not been fulfilled. Abraham was still forced to move around from place to place, since he did not have any land of his own.

One day, God decided to test Abraham. God told him to kill his son Isaac as a religious sacrifice. When the father and son arrived at the chosen site, Abraham bound Isaac and placed him upon an altar. As Abraham raised his knife, God sent an angel to stop him. God praised Abraham because he had not withheld his son, and sent a ram to take Isaac's place as the burnt offering. God then repeated the covenant promises to Abraham, and said that his children would become more numerous than the stars of heaven and the sand on the seashore.

Judaism views this incident, commonly referred to as the "binding of Isaac," as one of the most important events in Jewish history. This is because Abraham completely trusted in God's promise that his descendants would become the means through which all the nations of the world would be blessed. He was willing to give up his son to obey God. Both Christians and Muslims also view this incident as a foundational event in history, and regard Abraham's faith in God's promise as a model of perfect obedience that should be imitated today.

Abraham's wife, Sarah, died when she was 127 years old. Not only did Abraham grieve the loss of his wife, but he had no place to bury her. He went to a group of people in the land of Canaan known as the Hittites, who lived in a place called Hebron. Abraham asked them to sell him some land to use as a burial plot for his wife. After some discussion, they agreed, and sold him a plot of land that included a cave, trees, and a field. It was through this sad event that Abraham came to own some land for the first time. Today, a first-century A.D. tomb enclosure built by the Jewish King Herod the Great marks the site of the cave in Hebron where Sarah was buried. Abraham and some of his descendants were later buried in this cave, too. The site, now known as the Tomb of the Patriarchs, is still revered by contemporary Jews and Muslims, who continue to go there to pray and remember Abraham.

Modern scholars disagree about when Abraham lived. The Jewish Scriptures are the only ancient books that mention him, and there are no clear references to any known people or places that could help determine exactly when Abraham lived. Because of this, some modern scholars believe that these stories are not all historical, but that some are legendary tales that were made up about Abraham. According to this theory, biblical accounts about the ancient Jewish people are part historical and part fictional. Traditionally, Jews have believed that these stories are factual. It is important to view them as historically true, because they continue to shape Judaism today.

Despite scholarly disagreements concerning whether Abraham was a real person who actually did all the things that the Jewish Scriptures claim he did, it is certain that much of the information in the Bible about the patriarchs is based on fact. For example, Abraham's hometown of Ur did exist. It was excavated in the 1920s by British archaeologist C. Leonard Woolley. Ur was quite a large city. It contained buildings several stories high and had many massive, stepped pyramid temples called *ziggurats*. Archaeologists also discovered ancient texts written on clay that described life in Ur. This kind of evidence suggests that at least parts of the stories about Abraham are indeed accurate.

THE EXODUS (1200 B.C.?)

The remainder of the Book of Genesis recounts stories about Abraham's descendants: Isaac, Jacob, and Joseph. (According to the Bible, God also provided for Ishmael, Abraham's son by the maid Hagar. Modern-day Muslims trace their spiritual heritage to Ishmael and his descendants.) During the time of Joseph, famine struck Canaan once again. The Hebrews again moved to Egypt, where they prospered under the leadership of Joseph, who became a high-ranking official. Beginning with the time of Abraham's descendant Joseph, many Jews moved to Egypt to escape famine (Genesis 42:2). They stayed in the country for many generations and, presumably to pay for food, sold themselves into slavery. As slaves in Egypt, the Jews were forced to perform hard physical labor (Exodus 1:8–14).

Over time, relationships with the Egyptians and their king, called a *pharaoh*, became strained. The new pharaohs who ruled after Joseph's death did not favor the Hebrews. The Egyptians began to fear the Hebrews, because they were so numerous. It looked as if the Hebrews would never return to the land of Canaan that God had promised to Abraham's descendants.

The story of the departure of the Hebrews from Egypt is known as the Exodus. The Exodus is the most important event in Judaism, and is still commemorated by Jews around the world. *Exodus* is a Greek word that means "to leave" or "going out." It is also the name of one of the early books of the Bible, which tells the story of the Exodus. As with stories about Abraham, scholars disagree over the accuracy of many of the events described in the Book of Exodus. It is difficult to determine precisely when the Exodus occurred, because the Jewish Scriptures never name the pharaoh who ruled Egypt when it took place. Most scholars believe that the Exodus was an actual event, although they recognize that many of the biblical stories describing it were likely made up much later. Jews have traditionally regarded these accounts as true, just as they have all the other stories found in the Scriptures.

According to the Scriptures, the Hebrews were forced to build cities for the pharaohs. Two of these cities, Pithom and Rameses (Exodus 1:11), have possibly been uncovered by archaeologists, giving the likely date of the Exodus. They were built by the Egyptian Pharaoh Rameses II (1290–1224 B.C.). Because Rameses II named the city of Rameses after himself, many Jews and biblical scholars believe that the Exodus took place during his reign.

Whether it was indeed Rameses or not, the pharaoh was afraid that, because the Hebrews were so numerous, they would take over the country. To limit their numbers, he ordered that all male Hebrew children be put to death. A Hebrew woman defied this order, and attempted to save her son by placing him in a basket and setting it adrift in the Nile River. The pharaoh's daughter found the child and decided to adopt him. She named him Moses. When Moses became an adult, he saw an Egyptian beating a Hebrew. Feeling a connection with his own people, although he had been raised among Egyptians (Exodus 2:10), Moses grew angry and killed the Egyptian, hiding the dead man's body in the sand. When his crime was discovered, the pharaoh ordered that Moses be executed for the murder. Moses fled Egypt.

Moses eventually reached the desert of Midian, which is located in a region known as the Sinai Peninsula of Egypt. There, he married a woman named Zipporah, and became a shepherd, working with his father-in-law, Jethro.

One day, Moses was watching his flock on the mountain that is usually referred to as Sinai. Moses saw that a bush was on fire, burning, but was not being consumed by the flames. Moses became curious, and climbed farther up the mountain to see the bush more closely. God himself, in the visible form of an angel, appeared to Moses in the burning bush. God told Moses to come no closer, and to remove his sandals because he was standing upon holy ground. As the Bible explains, God said, "I am the God of your father, the God of Abraham, the God of Isaac, and the God of Jacob." Then Moses hid his face, for he was afraid to look at God. God then said, "I have surely seen the affliction of My people who are in Egypt, and have given heed to their cry because of their taskmasters, for I am aware of their sufferings" (Exodus 3:6–3:7). God told Moses that he would deliver the Hebrews from the Egyptians and bring them to a land flowing with milk and honey: the land of Canaan. God told Moses to return to Egypt and ask the pharaoh to let the Hebrews go into the desert to worship God.

God offered Moses a sign to prove that he would be with him: When Moses brought the people out of Egypt, they would worship God on the very mountain on which he was now standing. Moses then asked God to reveal his name, in case the Hebrews asked for the identity of the deity who had sent Moses to them. God said to Moses: "I Am Who I Am." He told Moses to tell the Hebrews: "I Am has sent me to you."

In Hebrew, the name "I Am Who I Am" consists of the four letters "YHWY" and is pronounced "Yahweh." It is called the *tetragram.* To show respect for God, Jews normally do not say this divine name when they pray or read the Bible. Instead, they replace the vowels of the name "Yahweh" with the vowels for the Hebrew word *Lord*, and say "Adonai." The Jewish people believe that God revealed his divine name to Moses to show the Hebrews that the covenant made with Abraham was still in effect.

Moses returned to Egypt and asked the pharaoh to let the Hebrews go into the desert to worship their God. The pharaoh refused, as God had warned Moses he would. God then sent ten miraculous plagues upon the Egyptians to convince them to release the Hebrews. In the first plague, the waters of the Nile turned into blood. The second was a plague of frogs that could be found everywhere, preventing normal life from going on. The third plague brought lice, which attacked the Egyptians and caused them severe itching and discomfort. The fourth plague brought massive waves of flies, thick enough to darken the skies. The fifth plague was a deadly pestilence that killed livestock in droves. The sixth plague caused the people to break out with terrible, painful boils. The seventh was a hailstorm that damaged everything in its path. The eighth plague, similar to the fourth, was a swarm of locusts. The ninth brought constant darkness. The final, tenth, plague caused the death of the firstborn of every house in Egypt. God told the Hebrews to smear lamb's blood on their doorposts, so the angel of death would pass over their homes and spare their children. God also commanded the Hebrews to celebrate this event each year by holding a commemorative meal to remember God's deliverance of the Hebrews from their bondage in Egypt. This meal of roasted lamb, bitter herbs, and unleavened bread is still celebrated by Jews around the world each year; it is called Passover.

After the last plague, the pharaoh finally agreed to release the Hebrews. He changed his mind after the Hebrews left Egypt, however. He sent an army to follow and destroy Moses and his people. The Egyptians trapped the Hebrews beside a body of water known as the "Sea of Reeds." This place was later mistranslated in English versions of the Bible as the "Red Sea." The "Sea of Reeds" was likely located north of the Red Sea where reeds called *papyrus* grew. According to the biblical account, God intervened to save the Hebrews by parting the waters, allowing them passage through the "Sea of Reeds." When the Egyptian Army tried to follow, the waters closed and the soldiers drowned. Moses and the Hebrews continued their journey to the mountain where Moses had seen the burning bush and heard the voice of God.

When the Hebrews reached Mount Sinai, Moses climbed alone to the top of the mountain to speak with God. There, God gave Moses a code of laws for the Hebrews to follow. The Hebrew word for "law" is *torah*. The name "Torah" refers to the laws that Moses received on Mount Sinai, along with the first five books of the Jewish Scriptures. The most important and famous part of the Torah is known as the Ten Commandments, also called the Decalogue. It is a list of ten laws that the Hebrews were required to follow. In the Jewish Scriptures, these laws are never actually called the "Ten Commandments." This is simply a name that people gave to the spiritual instructions God gave to Moses. Jews and Christians sometimes number the commandments differently, but they always include the same basic regulations and prohibitions:

1. You shall have no other gods before me.

2. You shall not make any graven images.

3. You shall not make any false oaths in God's name.

4. Remember the Sabbath day and keep it holy.

5. Honor your father and your mother.

6. You shall not commit murder.

7. You shall not commit adultery.

8. You shall not steal.

9. You shall not testify falsely against your neighbor.

10. You shall not covet your neighbor's property.

The Ten Commandments, which emphasize monotheism, are largely a series of prohibitions that tell the Hebrews what they are not supposed to do. The Hebrews were not allowed to make images of God. They were required to rest on the seventh day of the week, called the Sabbath, as a way to worship God. The other commandments regulated behavior in the Hebrew community.

In addition to the Ten Commandments, God gave Moses many other rules and regulations. For example, the Hebrews were forbidden to eat certain kinds of foods, such as pork, which God declared unclean. The biblical books of Exodus and Leviticus contain extensive commentaries on each of the Ten Commandments and how to fulfill them in daily life.

Many Jews consider Moses the most important figure in Jewish history because he received the laws that define and regulate Jewish life even in modern times. The Torah marks a major turning point in the religion of the Hebrews. Prior to Moses, the Hebrews had been expected to do very little other than practice circumcision and worship one God as part of their faith. After Moses, there were many laws to observe, such as the Sabbath day of rest, when Jews were forbidden to work, a practice that separated them from the other people of the area. The extensive code of laws was designed to remind Jews of God and to help them behave properly. Because all religions have beliefs, rules, and regulations that set them apart from other religions, many scholars say that the religion of Judaism begins with Moses and the Torah. This is because Moses is the traditional source of Judaism's unique lifestyle.

Moses became the religious and political leader of the Hebrews. God also commanded him to build a portable structure known as the Ark of the Covenant that represented God's presence in the Hebrews' camp. At God's command, Moses selected and ordained priests to supervise worship rituals and to protect the Ark of the Covenant. The Hebrews were also instructed to build a portable tent shrine, known as the Tabernacle, to house the Ark of the Covenant. This shrine was dismantled whenever God told the Hebrews to move, and reassembled when they were ordered to stop.

During their time in the desert, God protected the Hebrews and provided them with food. When they reached the land of Canaan, many refused to enter because they were afraid of the people who already lived there. Because of this disobedience, God punished the Hebrews by forcing them to live in the Sinai Desert for forty years. With the exception of two men, who were faithful to God, only children, who were not deemed responsible for angering God, were allowed to enter the land of Canaan before the forty years had passed. Because Moses had made God angry by showing an unwillingness to follow God's will and continue leading the Hebrews, he was told that he would not be permitted to enter Canaan. Moses was commanded to appoint a successor to lead the people.

Joshua, a military and political leader from the tribe of Ephraim, became the next leader of the Hebrews, and led them into the land of Canaan after the forty years had passed.

This turned out to be a very violent time in Jewish history. In fact, this period is known as the Conquest. The Hebrews fought the Canaanites because they believed that God had given them the land. Although the Hebrews managed to occupy much territory, and created what eventually became the nation of Israel, they were never able to remove the Canaanites from the land entirely. When the Hebrews failed to follow the Torah, God allowed the Canaanites to conquer them. When they repented, God sent leaders known as judges to save the Hebrews from their enemies. The period of the judges lasted for several generations, until the Hebrews asked God for a king to lead them.

THE MONARCHY (c. 1020–587 B.C.)

Over time, a new group of people, the Philistines, began to push the Hebrews out of their land. The Hebrews realized that they needed a king and a professional army if they hoped to defeat their enemies. God chose a man named Saul to govern the Hebrews and lead them in battle. Once, God sent Saul to conquer and destroy a neighboring people because they worshiped idols. Although Saul defeated his enemies, he did not kill the king and his subjects as God had ordered. Because of Saul's disobedience, he was replaced by a new king named David.

David, who was originally a shepherd, became famous for accepting the challenge to fight a Philistine giant named Goliath. Goliath had been mocking the Hebrew Army for some time, and wanted to fight the champion of the Hebrews in one-on-one combat. David was the only person who was willing to fight Goliath. Refusing to wear armor, David fought Goliath armed with only a slingshot and some stones. Despite the odds against him, David killed Goliath with a single stone. Because of his bravery, David rose rapidly in Saul's army. As David became more popular, Saul grew jealous. Saul became suspicious of David, and tried to kill him so that his own son Jonathan could become king. Saul and Jonathan were killed in a battle with the Philistines, and David became king of the Hebrews.

At this time, the Hebrews were divided into twelve different tribes. Each tribe traced its heritage to one of the twelve sons of the patriarch Joseph. The two southern tribes were called Judah, and the ten northern tribes were known as Israel. David united the twelve tribes and created the Nation of Israel. The Hebrews became known as the Israelites.

David built a new capital in the city called Jerusalem and brought the Ark of the Covenant there. According to the Jewish Scriptures, David, unlike Saul, sought God's forgiveness whenever he sinned. For this reason, God frequently punished David, but promised him that his sons would continue to rule in Jerusalem. This promise is sometimes referred to as the Davidic covenant.

David wanted to build a temple in Jerusalem to honor God. Although God denied David's request, God promised that David's son would build a temple one day. When David's son Solomon became king, he constructed an elaborate temple in Jerusalem. The Jerusalem Temple became the only place where the ancient Israelites were permitted to make sacrifices to God. Because Jerusalem was the site chosen for the Temple, it remains an important city for Jews today, even though the Temple itself was destroyed long ago.

After Solomon's death, the Nation of Israel divided and went through a lengthy period of civil war. The two southern tribes remained loyal to David's descendants, and became known as the Nation of Judah. The ten northern tribes rejected David's descendants and set up their own monarchy. They became known as the Nation of Israel.

During the period when the nation was divided, God sent people known as prophets to guide the Israelites. A prophet is a person who speaks on behalf of God. Prophets sometimes predicted the future and performed miracles. Preaching, however, was their main job. Unlike the priests, who supervised Temple rituals, the prophets were frequently outsiders.

They did not answer to the priests or the king. Prophets often denounced the people for disobeying God. The prophets always stressed that the Israelites should never abandon monotheism and must avoid idolatry. Because of their opposition to corrupt political and religious practices, most prophets were not treated well by the people.

The southern Nation of Judah survived longer than the northern Nation of Israel because it remained loyal to David's descendants. The kingship was never in doubt in Judah, because everyone agreed that the monarch had to be a Davidic descendant. The northern Nation of Israel, on the other hand, frequently fought wars to determine who would become king. Israel was destroyed by the Assyrians in 721 B.C. The Assyrians, who controlled a large territory that stretched from Mesopotamia to Turkey, took many of the Israelites away into exile, scattering them all over the Assyrian Empire. Over time, these people intermarried and adopted the customs of the Assyrians; eventually, they were no longer Israelites. They lost their religious identity and became polytheists. These ten tribes are sometimes called the "Lost Tribes of Israel" because they disappeared from history entirely.

Judah continued to be ruled by David's descendants until 587 B.C., when the Babylonians, who came from the land that is now Iraq, forcibly removed the last Davidic king. The Babylonians took many of the people of Judah into Babylon to prevent them from uniting and revolting. The Babylonians also destroyed the Jerusalem Temple.

Many important religious aspects of Judaism began during the Exile. The loss of the Temple in Jerusalem forced the Jews to reexamine their relationship with God. It was the prophets, such as Ezekiel, who helped the people cope with the Exile. The prophets told the Jews that God was everywhere, and could be worshipped anywhere, even in Babylon. The Temple itself was not necessary for the people to worship God. Because God had commanded that sacrifices take place only in the Jerusalem Temple, however, the people who lived in exile began to write and collect the Scriptures instead of making sacrifices. The study of these texts replaced sacrifice as a form of worship. Judaism became a religion that was based on a book. During this time, the people of Judah became known as Jews, and the land of Canaan was called Israel.

After the collapse of the Babylonian Empire, the Jews were allowed to return to Jerusalem. Although they rebuilt the Jerusalem Temple, it was never as important as it had been in the past. Jews could visit Jerusalem and make sacrifices to God if they chose. Most Jews, however, lived too far from Jerusalem to visit the Temple. They simply prayed and studied the Jewish Scriptures in order to worship God. The word *Diaspora* refers to Jews who lived outside the land of Israel. Most Jews today are still considered part of the Diaspora.

JEHOVAH: THE GOD THAT DOES NOT EXIST

In the Tanakh, God tells Moses that his name is "YHWH." Ancient Hebrew was not written with any vowels; only the consonants were written. Over time, people began to forget how to pronounce Hebrew as their ancestors did. It was not until much later in the Common Era (A.D.) that vowels were added. Because Jews did not want to make errors in the original Hebrew and Aramaic languages of the Tanakh, they placed the vowels as dots and dashes above and below the consonants to show that they had been added to the original.

To show respect for God, Jews did not pronounce the divine name of God, "YHWH." Instead, they substituted the Hebrew word for "Lord," *Adonai*, whenever they read the Tanakh. To remind readers not to pronounce the name of God, the written text contained the consonants of "YHWH," but placed the vowels of *Adonai* above and beneath the word *YHWH*. Because this word does not exist, the reader immediately knew to replace *YHWH* with *Adonai*. In A.D. 1270, Christians who did not know this tradition mistakenly began to read the consonants of "YHWH" and the vowels of "Adonai" together, and pronounced God's name as "Jehovah." The word *Jehovah* is a mistaken combination of the consonants of "YHWH" with the vowels of "Adonai." Although the word *Jehovah* never existed, it is still found in many contemporary Christian hymns.

A RELIGION TO PRACTICE ANYWHERE

There are several important people and events that make up the foundation for the religion that eventually developed into contemporary Judaism. Abraham, Moses, David, Solomon, and the prophets collectively make up Judaism's founders. Abraham received the covenant, which Jews believe is still in effect. The covenant promised that the Jews would have an ongoing relationship with God. Moses received the Torah that distinguished the Jews from the people around them and created and defined Judaism's ethical system and ritual practices, many of which continue to the present day. David received a promise that his descendants would govern Jerusalem forever. The prophets looked to the future, when God would send a figure known as the Messiah to restore the Davidic kingship. This is because of the biblical promise that David's descendants, from whom the Messiah would descend, will sit upon the throne of Jerusalem forever (2 Samuel 7). Since there are no Davidic kings, some Jews believe that the promises of the Messiah have been fulfilled spiritually, whereas others still take them literally and expect a Messiah to come.

During the Exile, the Jewish community put its history and teachings about God down in writing. These texts became the Jewish Scriptures, which remain the basis for Judaism even now. Judaism after the Exile became a universal religion that could be practiced anywhere. Although the Jerusalem Temple had been rebuilt about two hundred years after the Babylonians destroyed it, in A.D. 70, the Romans invaded Israel and destroyed the Temple again. It has never been rebuilt. Because of the Exile, however, this event did not eradicate Judaism. The Exile had brought about a spiritual understanding of the Jewish Scriptures that has remained in effect ever since. The Exile created a model for modernizing and adapting Judaism to new historical circumstances. Jews were simply required to pray to the one God, to study the Jewish Scriptures, and to follow the basic laws and ethical system of Judaism wherever they lived.

3

The Jewish Scriptures

*Now the Lord said to Moses, "Come up to Me on
the mountain and remain there, and I will give you
the stone tablets with the law and the commandment
which I have written for their instruction."*

—Exodus 24:12

J ews have traditionally learned about God by studying the written word. For this reason, Judaism is a religion that stresses the study of the Jewish Scriptures and other Jewish texts—a religion of the book. Because God created the world, Judaism encourages other areas of study, such as science, because they, too, can teach us about God's creation.

All Jews today, despite their differences, revere the stories and history that are recorded in the Jewish Scriptures. Judaism is a revealed religion. It teaches that God has intervened in history to protect and guide the Jewish people. Jews also believe that God has revealed these teachings to messengers, in the words of the prophets, and that these were collected in the Jewish Scriptures. These Scriptures became the basis for the religion of Judaism. They describe the foundational beliefs and practices of the faith. Although they where written by humans, Jews have traditionally considered the Jewish Scriptures God's word and believe they are divine.

THE TANAKH

Before the Exile, Judaism was primarily an oral religion. During the Exile, Jews began to collect the teachings of their prophets, and writings about their ancestors. Since then, Judaism has become a religion based on scripture. According to some ancient Jewish traditions, a man named Ezra was largely responsible for collecting the Jewish Scriptures during the Exile.

The Jewish Bible is actually a library of many books that consists of three parts: Torah, Writings, and Prophets. Jews in the past simply referred to these books as the *Bible*, which is a Greek translation of the Hebrew word for "book." They also took the first letter of the Hebrew name for each of these three divisions of the Bible and inserted vowels to come up with the acronym *Tanakh*. Jews commonly use the word *Tanakh* to refer to their Scriptures. Some Jews also call the Tanakh the Hebrew Bible, because the majority of these books were written in Hebrew. A few books of the Jewish Scriptures were written in Aramaic, which is a language that is related to Hebrew.

The Jewish Scriptures are unique among the sacred texts of the world's religions, because they form the basis for the holy books of other faiths. Christianity accepts the Jewish Scriptures as the word of God. The Christian faith is based on the teachings of a Jew named Jesus, who lived in Israel during the first century A.D. Jesus frequently quoted from the Jewish Scriptures and taught people how to live according to his interpretation of them. Jesus's followers believed he was the Messiah who had been foretold in the Scriptures. The Romans crucified Jesus because they feared that his followers wanted him to become king.

A GOAT DISCOVERS THE WORLD'S OLDEST COPY OF THE TANAKH

For centuries, the Bedouin of the Ta'amireh tribe have roamed along the Dead Sea in modern Israel, seeking forage and water for their flocks of sheep and goats. One day during the winter of 1946–1947, three members of the Ta'amireh tribe were herding their goats beside the Dead Sea. Shepherd Muhammed edh-Dhib noticed that one goat was missing. In its search for food, the stray goat had scaled the craggy rocks of the adjacent cliffs and wandered into a cave. While try-ing to retrieve the animal, Muhammed noticed a small hole among the rocks, barely large enough for a cat to enter. Muhammed threw a stone into this opening, and was quite surprised to hear the sound of shattering pottery. Believing that the cave was full of gold, Muhammed squeezed through the narrow crevice in search of treasure. He saw approximately ten jars set along the cave's walls. Muhammed removed the lids of these mysterious jars to examine the contents, and was disappointed to find that they contained not gold, but seven old scrolls wrapped in colored cloth. One of these scrolls was a complete copy from the Tanakh of the Book of Isaiah, which had been copied in the second century B.C. These scrolls, now known as the Dead Sea Scrolls, contain the world's oldest copies of the Tanakh. Unfortunately, the name of the goat that discovered the Dead Sea Scrolls was never recorded, and has been lost to history.

For this story, see Kenneth Atkinson, "Two Dogs, a Goat and a Partridge: An Archaeologist's Best Friends," *Biblical Archaeology Review* 22 (1996), pp. 42–43, 74.

After his death, the Christians wrote books about Jesus and formed their own book of scripture. Because Christians realized that their religion had emerged from Judaism, they attached their writings to the original Jewish Scriptures. Christians began to refer to the Jewish Scriptures as the "Old Testament," and to their own writings as the "New Testament." The word *testament* is Latin for "covenant." Christians called the Jewish Scriptures the Old Testament, because they viewed these writings as God's first covenant with humans. The New Testament, for Christians, contains God's new teachings, or covenant, which began with Jesus. Most Jews today do not use the name "Old Testament," because it is a Christian term.

When the religion of Islam was founded in the early seventh century A.D., it, too, accepted the teachings of the Old Testament. The Qur'an (or Koran), the sacred book of Islam, like the New Testament, frequently quotes from the Tanakh. The Tanakh, therefore, is unique, because it represents the basis for the world's three great monotheistic religions: Judaism, Christianity, and Islam.

The Jewish Tanakh is sometimes difficult to understand. This is because each of the many books has a long and complicated history. Many are actually collections of ancient material that was passed down through the generations orally before being put into writing. Each book of the Tanakh was copied onto ancient paper that was either made of reeds called papyrus or animal skin called parchment. The books were copied by hand. Sometimes, scribes added new material to these texts. The Book of Isaiah, for example, had to have been written by at least three writers, because it describes three different historical periods. Most scholars believe that the Jewish Scriptures reached their present form sometime around 400 B.C. The Jewish Scriptures are not arranged in chronological order. Rather, they are divided into three sections, known as the Torah, the Prophets, and the Writings.

TORAH

The first five books of the Jewish Scriptures are called the *Torah*, which is a Hebrew word that means "law." The Torah begins with a book called Genesis. This book tells about the creation of the universe and the history of the first humans. Genesis also contains the early history of the Jewish people, and stories about Abraham and his descendants Isaac, Jacob, and Joseph. Because Genesis contains writings about the covenant with Abraham, it is one of Judaism's most important books. It ends with a description of Abraham's descendants living in Egypt.

The second book of the Torah is simply called the Book of Exodus, because it tells the story about the departure, or exodus, of Moses and the Hebrews from Egypt. It contains many laws, also called Torah, which Moses received on Mount Sinai. The most famous of these are the Ten Commandments.

Leviticus, the third book of the Torah, is a detailed set of instructions about how to worship God. It includes many rules that tell Jews which foods they are permitted to eat. These regulations about which foods are ritually clean or acceptable are known as the laws of *kashrut*, or Jewish dietary laws.

The Book of Numbers continues the story of the Exodus, and recounts the wandering of the Jews in the wilderness of Sinai. Deuteronomy, the final book of the Torah, is an extended sermon by Moses. It warns about the consequences of forsaking the one God.

PROPHETS

The Prophets make up the second division of the Tanakh. The prophetic books are traditionally divided into Former and Latter Prophets. The earlier, or Former, Prophets include the books of Joshua, Judges, I and II Samuel, and I and II Kings. These books tell the history of the Jewish community from the time of Moses's successor, Joshua, until the return of the Jewish people to Jerusalem after the Exile. Although these books are largely historical accounts of the Jewish people, they are included among the Prophets because they contain many stories about the Prophets who guided the Jewish people.

The "Latter Prophets" consist of many books about the lives and work of the Jewish prophets. The first three books of the Latter Prophets include the teachings of the three greatest prophets of Judaism: Isaiah, Jeremiah, and Ezekiel. Each prophet has a book devoted to his teachings that also bears his name. The books of Isaiah, Jeremiah, and Ezekiel are also known as the Major Prophets, because of their length. They primarily include stories and sermons denouncing idolatry and violations of the Torah. Some, such as the Book of Isaiah, were written by more than one person. The remaining twelve books are known as the Minor Prophets, because they are short in length. They include: Hosea, Joel, Amos, Obadiah, Jonah, Micah, Nahum, Habakkuk, Zephaniah, Haggai, Zechariah, and Malachi. Sometimes the twelve Minor Prophets are called "The Book of the Twelve."

WRITINGS

The Writings are a collection of several different types of literature. The first is a book of poems known as Psalms. Most of the Psalms are attributed to King David. Proverbs and the Book of Job deal with the theme of wisdom. According to tradition, King David's son Solomon wrote Proverbs. The "Song of Songs" is a love poem about a man and a woman. Jews have understood this book as a symbolic story about God's relationship with Israel. Ecclesiastes is another wisdom book that examines whether there is any meaning in life. "Lamentations" is a poem about the destruction of Jerusalem and the temple by the Babylonian Army. According to Jewish tradition, the prophet Jeremiah wrote the poem. The Book of Esther is a story about a Jewish woman who saved her people from annihilation by a Persian king. Daniel is about a Jew named Daniel who was taken into exile. It begins with several stories about Daniel and his fellow captives, who struggled to practice their religion in exile. The second half of the Book of Daniel is a series of visions about the end of time.

The remaining books in the Writings are works of history. Ezra and Nehemiah recount the return of the Jewish people from exile in Babylon to Jerusalem, and the rebuilding of the Temple. The last two books of the Writings, I and II Chronicles, are similar to I and II Kings. They are about the history of the Jewish people from after Moses's time to the end of the Exile. The difference is that I and II Chronicles, unlike I and II Kings, focuses on the Jerusalem Temple and the priests.

VERSIONS OF THE TANAKH

When the Tanakh was written, there was no such thing as a book. The books of the Bible were originally written on scrolls, the ancestor of the modern book. A scroll consists of sheets of paper made of papyrus or parchment that were sewn together. A scroll was very long, and had to be unrolled as it was read. In order to maintain a connection with their past, modern-day Jews still copy some of their holy books on scrolls for use in worship.

When Christians adopted the Tanakh, they counted each part as a separate book and arranged them differently. They placed the Prophets last, because these texts talk about the Messiah. For Christians, the rearranged Old Testament is incomplete, because it ends with an expectation that the Messiah will come. The Jewish Tanakh, however, ends with the historical books of Ezra, Nehemiah, and I and II Chronicles, which tell about the return from Exile and the rebuilding of Jerusalem. Unlike the Christian Old Testament, the Jewish Tanakh begins with creation and ends on a happy note, since it describes how Judaism survived the trauma of the Exile. These differences show how the books of the Tanakh, although accepted by Jews, Christians, and Muslims, can be reordered to convey very different theological messages.

THE MISHNAH

For centuries, the Tanakh remained the basic book of Judaism. When Jews had questions, they looked to the Tanakh as the inspired word of God for answers. Because their lifestyle had not changed, the Tanakh answered all their questions. Over time, though, as more Jews began to live in the Diaspora, they began to have new questions about how to practice Judaism that were not covered in the Bible. Jewish religious leaders and preachers, called rabbis, were frequently called upon to determine how to apply the Torah in the Bible to new situations.

Following the destruction of the Jerusalem Temple by the Romans in A.D. 70, the rabbis replaced the priests as Jewish spiritual leaders. The central question then was how to practice the Judaism of the Tanakh without the Temple. Although biblical stories about the Exile provided a model for being Jewish in the absence of the Temple, Jews had many questions about which laws in the Torah were still binding. The rabbis would frequently meet to discuss Jewish laws and give their opinions about how to practice Judaism. They began to document many of their interpretations and record stories about how their ancestors had practiced Judaism prior to the Temple's destruction. Although the rabbis realized that the Temple was not likely to be rebuilt soon, they thought it was important to preserve any stories about the ancient Jerusalem Temple to help them understand their history.

At first, the opinions of the rabbis circulated orally. Over time, however, many Jews came to regard the teachings and interpretations of the rabbis as another form of scripture. The rabbis taught that there were two types of Torah: written and oral. The Tanakh is the Written Torah. It is the written record of God's laws, and the history of the Jewish people. According to Jewish belief, the Oral Torah contains additional laws that God gave to Moses at Mount Sinai. These laws, however, were not given to the people as a whole. They were memorized and passed down orally through successive generations of rabbis.

According to Jewish tradition, the Written Torah and the Oral Torah are equally valuable. The Oral Torah and its interpretations by the rabbis were written down about A.D. 200 in a book known as the *Mishnah.*

Judaism underwent many changes from the time of Abraham to the end of the Exile. The rabbis of the Mishnah saw themselves in continuity with the past, yet wanted to modernize Judaism. Jews considered the Mishnah another chapter in God's unfolding plan for humanity. Because the biblical covenant promise that King David's descendants would always sit upon the throne in Jerusalem (2 Samuel 7) had not been fulfilled, some people, both Jews and Gentiles, challenged the traditional understanding of the covenant and said that it was no longer in effect. For this reason, many Jews began to interpret such passages symbolically to maintain that God had not violated the covenant. The Mishnah was another book that helped Jews live as part of the covenant community.

Over the years, the rabbis began to study and debate the teachings recorded in the Mishnah. They also began to collect two other types of literature: *haggadah* and *halakhah.* Haggadah includes narrative and other nonlegal writings. It contains stories about the Jewish people, as well as tales told for entertainment and instruction. Halakhah (also spelled as *halachah*) includes traditions, opinions, and discussions about Jewish law. The kosher laws of food, such as the prohibition against eating pork, are examples of halakhah. The haggadah and halakhah were eventually put together in many books that were collectively called the *Gemara.* The combination of the Mishnah and the Gemara is known as the *Talmud.*

THE TALMUD

The Talmud was written over an extended period of time by rabbis who lived in Palestine and Babylon. Each of these two communities produced its own version of the Talmud. The first was written in Palestine around A.D. 425, and is called the Palestinian Talmud. This version was replaced by the

Babylonian Talmud, which was completed around A.D. 500. Unless otherwise specified, the word *Talmud* always refers to the Babylonian Talmud.

The Talmud includes history, folklore, and sermons. Jews do not consider the Talmud divinely inspired scripture. Rather, it is a repository of Jewish tradition, designed to serve as a guide for future generations. It teaches members of the faith how to live and think like Jews.

Academies of learning were established that were similar to modern universities. Each was led by a president called a *Gaon* ("Excellency"). Because many Jews followed the teachings and interpretations of these academies, the period between A.D 600 and 1000 is sometimes known as the Gaonic Period. The title *Gaon* was later used as a title of respect for a scholar of the Talmud.

The rabbis who produced the Talmud, like their predecessors who had collected the traditions preserved in the Mishnah, tried to provide a model for being Jewish. Judaism has always tolerated diversity. There have always been differences within the Jewish community. Even the rabbis of the Talmud disagreed with one another. Although they all tried to follow the ancient Jewish laws, they did not always agree about how those laws should be interpreted and practiced. The rabbis of the Talmud looked to the Mishnah and came up with a solution: to encourage diversity. Much of the Talmud is a series of religious debates, of which all sides are recorded. The rabbis at the time of the Talmud usually agreed to follow the majority opinion, but they still wrote down divergent views in case they became useful later. Because the Talmud recorded many diverse opinions, it became a model for Judaism.

Jews traditionally study the Talmud by debating an opponent. The object of such debates, however, is not to win. Rather, the aim is to learn how to be righteous. Sometimes students will switch sides during the debate, in order to learn how to think.

The Talmud remains the most important book of Judaism

besides the Tanakh, even to the present day. Many modern editions of the Talmud include the teachings of later rabbis in the margins.

JEWISH MYSTICISM

Between A.D. 500 and 900, many Jews began to write down mystical interpretations of the Tanakh and the Talmud. For these Jews, the Tanakh and Talmud had an inner meaning. Although the obvious meaning of these books is important, for the mystics, the hidden truths were even more profound. Mystics concentrated on angels, demons, magical spells, and charms.

Jewish mysticism is called *Kabbalah*. The major book of the Kabbalah is known as the *Zohar*, sometimes referred to as the Book of Splendor. According to tradition, the Zohar was written during the second century A.D. by a Jewish leader named Simeon bar Yohai. Most scholars believe that the Zohar was actually written by Moses de Leon, who was a thirteenth-century Spanish mystic from Córdoba. It contains many descriptions of visions, and emphasizes the presence of God (called the *Shekhinah* in Hebrew) in the world.

Kabbalism views the Shekhinah as the female aspect of God. According to the Kabbalah, human souls are divine sparks that were created as the result of an accident. Divine vessels accidentally spewed evil into the world, as well as fragments of divine light. This traumatic event destroyed God's plan for the Creation. Humans have an obligation to help God restore the divine sparks in their souls to the sacred vessels. This correction, or repair, of the present human condition is known as *tikkun*. In some forms of Jewish mysticism, prayers and ritual practices can help God repair the broken vessels of divine light.

Kabbalism also emphasizes the interpretation of *gematria*, which is the practice of transposing words into numbers. Ancient Hebrew had no numbers. Instead, each letter had a numerical value, and could be used as a number. Kabbalah adds up the numerical value of the words in the Tanakh and other Jewish texts to uncover their mystical significance.

The Kabbalah became popular with Jews when they were being persecuted during the Middle Ages. Some scholars believe that Jews who lived under normal circumstances developed the Talmud, whereas the literature of the Kabbalah emerged within oppressed Jewish communities that had little hope for the future. In recent decades, there has been a resurgence of interest in the teachings of the Kabbalah. In Israel, the ancient city of Safed is a center for the study of the Kabbalah.

4

Worldview

And the Lord said to Abram . . .
"Now lift up your eyes and look from the place
where you are, northward and southward and eastward
and westward; for all the land which you see, I will give
it to you and to your descendants forever."

—Genesis 13:14–15

Judaism is a difficult religion to define, in part because it has existed for thousands of years. Over the centuries, the religion of Judaism has changed considerably. Jews have adapted and altered many of their beliefs and worship practices. Some changes were made in accordance with the Jewish community's new understandings of God. For example, many contemporary Jews no longer follow the ancestral kosher food laws because they believe they are no longer essential. Other changes were forced upon the Jewish community. In the modern era, Jews who wanted to follow their ancestral traditions have had to reconcile ancient practices with modernity and technology. Despite Judaism's changes over time, a few traditional beliefs continue to be part of the Jewish worldview today.

GOD

Judaism does not require its followers to agree upon a particular creed. Jews have always been allowed to disagree about certain beliefs. The Jewish religion, however, is based on monotheism, which is the belief in one God. Jews believe that there is a single creator God, who is the source of everything. During worship, many Jews recite a statement of belief in one God known as the *Shema*, which is a Hebrew word that means "Hear" or "Listen." The Shema is a passage that comes from the Jewish Scriptures. It reads: "Hear O Israel? The Lord our God, the Lord is one. You shall love the Lord your God with all your heart, with all your soul, and with all your might." This passage expresses the Jewish belief that there is only a single God who is everywhere at once.

God's divine presence, called the *Shekhinah* in Hebrew, fills heaven and Earth. Humans, moreover, are created in the image of God. Because of this, Judaism teaches that all life is sacred. Because God is the source of everything, God cannot fully be understood. As a result, Judaism has traditionally avoided creating depictions of God. Jews have generally considered such images idolatry. Today, Jewish places of worship, called synagogues, do not contain pictures or other representations of God.

Throughout the history of Judaism, Jewish thinkers and theologians have sought to explain God. Like other religions that believe in one God, such as Christianity and Islam, Judaism has found it difficult to describe God. This is because God is beyond human understanding. Judaism has always understood its sacred texts, such as the Tanakh, to contain only metaphors, not literal truths, about God. A metaphor is a figure of speech. Jewish texts were written in language that was familiar to people in order to teach them about God. Scriptural language is intended to describe God's qualities. For example, when the Jewish Scriptures say "the Lord is my shepherd," this does not mean that God is actually a shepherd. In this case, God, like a shepherd, watches over his flock (the Jews) to protect them from harm. When Jews in the past saw shepherds walking through the fields of Israel with their flocks of sheep, they were reminded of God's care and protection.

MAIMONIDES'S THIRTEEN PRINCIPLES

Jews today continue to look to the Tanakh to understand God. The famous Jewish theologian Moses Maimonides (1135–1204) tried to simplify Jewish teachings about God so that they would be easier to understand and remember. He identified thirteen foundational principles of faith. Jews frequently refer to Maimonides's list to explain the Jewish conception of God. Maimonides's principles are:

1. God is the Creator.

2. God is One.

3. God does not have a physical form.

4. God is eternal.

5. God alone is to be worshipped.

6. God has revealed his will through the prophets of the Jewish Scriptures.

7. Moses is the greatest prophet.

8. God revealed the Torah to Moses.

9. The Torah is eternal and never changes.

10. God knows everything.

11. God rewards and punishes all humans.

12. God will send the Messiah.

13. There is a resurrection of the dead.

Maimonides's first five principles deal with God's nature. They emphasize that there is only one God, who is the source of everything. To worship anything or anyone other than God is idolatry. Judaism does not allow polytheism.

Maimonides's next four principles describe God's relationship with the Jewish people. These stories about the history of the Jews and the prophets are found in the Tanakh, and begin with Moses, who received God's laws, the Torah. Judaism has always considered the Torah special. Jews believe that Moses was the greatest of God's prophets, because he was chosen to receive the Torah. Over time, many Jews began to teach that the Torah, because it came from God, is perfect like God. Because God is eternal and never changes, many Jews began to believe that the Torah, too, was perpetually unchanging. The Torah is, in effect, a mirror of God that teaches humans about God through words. By following the rules and teachings of the Torah, Jews are brought closer to God. In the modern period, many Jews have stopped practicing the lifestyle advocated in the Torah; even so, they still revere the Torah as a document of their faith that contains the Jewish community's understanding of God.

The final four principles of Maimonides concern God's relationship with humans. Judaism teaches that God knows everything, and will reward and punish all humans for their good and bad deeds. Judaism has traditionally taught that God will send a figure, called the Messiah, who would put an end to evil, rebuild the Temple, bring the exiles back to Israel, and usher in the new world to come. The Hebrew word *messiah* means "anointed one," which refers to the ancient practice of anointing kings with oil when they took office. Judaism used the term to refer to the future person who would be chosen to and guide the Jewish people. Jews today disagree about the Messiah. Some believe that he will come in the future, while others no longer expect a Messiah. Unlike Christians, most Jews do not recognize Jesus as the Messiah, although many do admire his ethical teachings, which are similar to those of Judaism. Jesus was Jewish and came to be regarded by some Jews of his day as the Messiah. When Christians wrote their own book of Scriptures, the New Testament, they wanted to emphasize Christianity's connection with Judaism, so they stressed that Jesus was the Messiah who had been predicted in the Jewish Scriptures. The Christian New Testament, which was written in Greek, calls Jesus the "Christ," which is a translation of the Hebrew word *messiah*.

JEWISH TOLERANCE FOR OTHER FAITHS

Judaism is a universal religion. It can be practiced anywhere, because it believes that God is everywhere. In the faith's early days, described in the Tanakh, the first Jews lived in the area that is now Israel. Judaism was largely restricted to this geographical region. The Tanakh, however, teaches that God chose the Jewish people to bless all humanity. For this reason, Judaism has always understood itself as a religion that is not just for Jews, but one that seeks to help all people.

For most of their faith's history, the Jews have not had their own country, and have lived as a minority among non-Jews. This was possible because Judaism has always taught that God is always with the Jewish people.

Despite the many different types of modern Judaism, all Jews believe that they are connected to the ancient Jews who wrote the Tanakh and other Jewish religious texts in an effort to understand

God. Like their spiritual ancestors, modern Jews believe they are constantly struggling to learn how best to live as Jews. Judaism has taught that, although the Jewish people may on occasion desert their God, God will never abandon the Jewish people.

THE COVENANT

Judaism teaches that God chose to establish a covenant with Abraham, the "Father of the Jews." This is why the Jewish people are sometimes referred to as "the chosen people." The covenant was a contract between God and Abraham and his descendants, based on monotheism. God promised Abraham a certain parcel of land, many descendants, and that all nations would be blessed through him. Circumcision was the sign of God's covenant with Abraham.

Most Jews believe that the covenant is still in effect, and that the religion of Judaism has a role to play in the healing of the world. Because Judaism teaches that people can never fully understand God, the covenant has always been regarded as a mystery. Judaism does not teach that good things will always happen to the Jews because of the covenant. Rather, the major blessing of the covenant is Judaism's close relationship with God. The Jewish covenant rests on faith—a belief in an omnipotent and omniscient God who is good, and who wants to maintain a relationship with the Jewish people.

THEODICY

Theodicy (which literally means "God's justice") attempts to explain good and evil. Put simply, it is a way to defend the idea that God is good even though he allows evil to exist in the world. Early Judaism did not have much of a concept of an afterlife. It later developed a belief in heaven, hell, and resurrection. (Resurrection, which is also an important concept in Christianity, refers to the raising of the dead in some form.) During the Exile, Judaism began to teach that people would be held accountable for their sins, and would be punished and rewarded accordingly on the Day of Judgment at the end of the world.

The Jewish belief in an afterlife emerged in part out of efforts to explain the origin of evil. Judaism and the other Western religions struggle with the problem of evil: How can evil exist if God is really omnipotent and good? The faith of Zoroastrianism first developed the concept of Satan (or the devil) to explain evil. During the Exile, Judaism adopted this same belief. Judaism traditionally teaches that Satan is God's adversary, who tempted the first humans to disobey God. Satan, however, does not appear in the biblical stories about the first humans. He is only mentioned in the latter books of the Tanakh. Judaism believes that God's goodness will eventually triumph over Satan and evil.

Judaism has traditionally viewed the creation as good because God is good. Evil is the absence of goodness and the consequence of sin. Judaism teaches that God gave humans complete freedom of choice—to choose to be good or evil. This means that humans, not God, are ultimately responsible for evil, because they choose to separate themselves from God by sinning. Satan cannot be used as an excuse for not being a righteous person. All people will be held accountable to God after death for their own conduct on Earth.

Many Jews began to question this traditional explanation of God's relationship to evil. Since the Holocaust, some Jews have tried to support the traditional Jewish view of the theodicy and maintain that God is good. Others believe that the God of the Tanakh, who is omnipotent and good, does not exist. They argue that the Jewish people must look to their community of faith for meaning. According to this interpretation, Judaism is a cultural heritage; Jews can still follow the values of Judaism, but are not required to adhere to the traditional laws of the Bible and Talmud. Another post-Holocaust explanation holds that God is in the world, and suffers along with humanity.

These questions about whether God is responsible for evil have always been a part of Judaism. The relationship between God and evil is really a question that grows out of a strictly monotheistic worldview. If God is the only source of all that is, then God must create evil as well as good.

In the Tanakh, Abraham not only questioned God, but even argued with God, trying to convince God not to destroy the cities of Sodom and Gomorrah. Despite this apparent lack of obedience, God chose to give the covenant to Abraham. According to the Bible, Abraham was a righteous man even though he challenged God. Judaism views itself as a community that has an ongoing relationship—and struggle—with God. Although Judaism has traditionally emphasized faith in God's justice, it struggled to understand God's will. Just as there are many answers to the question of who is a Jew, there are several Jewish explanations for the problem of evil.

THE TORAH

The word *Torah* refers broadly to the entire Jewish Bible, and more specifically, to the first five books of the Bible. Jewish tradition holds that Moses wrote these first five books. The Torah is the foundational text of Judaism, and the most important part of the Tanakh. The central teaching of the Torah is that there is only one God, who is both creator and redeemer. The first sentence of the Torah proclaims that God created the universe, and there is nothing in the universe greater than God.

The Torah also teaches that God is not a spirit that lives in nature; God is greater than nature. Judaism does not believe that nature should be worshiped, because it does not possess any divine attributes. God created everything in the cosmos, but only humans are made in the image of God. The Torah teaches that humans are therefore closer to God than anything else in the universe is. Judaism understands this to mean that humans have an obligation to be like God; they must practice justice and mercy. However, the Torah does not teach Jews to abandon civilization in order to worship God. Rather, it encourages people to enjoy life and to make every moment in life sacred. The role of humanity, according to Jewish tradition, is to bring justice and the knowledge of God to the world.

Judaism has traditionally taught that there are 613 commandments, called *mitzvoth*, in the Torah. Many biblical mitzvoth deal with social justice. Jews are commanded to help other people, to support charity, and to respect all life. The prophet Micah summarized the essence of the Torah when he asked, "What does God require of you but to do justice, love goodness, and walk righteously with God?"

The Torah teaches that God has intervened in history on behalf of the Jewish community. Few Jews believe that God still intervenes in history as he did in the time of the Bible, when the "Sea of Reeds" was parted and other miracles occurred. Because such events no longer take place, most contemporary Jews believe that God no longer directly intervenes in the world.

PROPHECY

During the time of the ancient Israelite monarchy, the prophets were the primary messengers of God. The prophets believed that God controlled history, rewarded obedience, and punished disobedience. The prophets interpreted Israel's history through their understandings of God and the Torah. They thought that when something bad happened to Israel, it was because the nation had disobeyed God in some way. However, the prophets also brought a message of hope. They said that God's love

ASHER GINSBERG (1856–1927) ON WHY WE ARE JEWISH

Nobody asked us before we were born, Do you want to be Jews? Do you like the teachings of Judaism, the Torah of Judaism? Judaism introduced us into its covenant without our knowledge or consent and gave us a completed Torah that preceded our own creation. . . . Why are we Jews? How strange the very question! . . . Ask the tree why it grows! . . . It is within us; it is one of our laws of nature. It has an existence and a constancy of its own, like a mother's love for her children, like a man's love of his homeland.

Quoted in Robert M. Seltzer, *Jewish People, Jewish Thought: The Jewish Experience in History.* New York: MacMillan, 1980, pp. 688–689.

was everlasting: If the Jews returned to God and followed the commandments, God would forgive their sins.

Some prophets spoke of the Messiah, saying that God would someday anoint a new king, a descendant of King David. This leader would usher in a new era of peace and justice. However, many contemporary Jews reject this traditional interpretation. They believe that the Messiah is a symbol of the hopes of the Jewish people and not a literal person. This is because biblical promises, such as the statement that King David's descendants, the family from which the Messiah will come, will sit on the throne in Jerusalem, have not been fulfilled. For this reason, many Jews interpret such promises, which seem to have gone unfulfilled, spiritually and no longer believe in a literal Messiah. Reform Jews believe that the Messianic Age promised in the Bible is a symbol of a future in which all humanity will be united.

SOCIAL JUSTICE

Social justice has always been a central teaching of Judaism, one that many of the prophets considered the most important part of the Torah. The prophet Amos, for example, denounced those who mistreated the poor. He believed that the covenant was a special blessing that had been given to the Jews and demanded that all Jews help other people when they were in need.

Because God gave the Jewish people the covenant and the Torah, Judaism has taught that the Jews have a special obligation to practice justice and mercy. The prophet Hosea even told the Israelites that God was not interested in sacrifice. Rather, God only desired love. This interpretation of the Torah enabled Judaism to survive after the Temple was destroyed and there could be no more sacrifice.

5

House of Worship:
A Visit to a Jewish Synagogue

*And behold, I intend to build a house for the name of
the Lord my God, as the Lord spoke to David my father,
saying, "Your son, whom I will set on your throne in
your place, he will build the house for My name."*

—1 Kings 5:5

J udaism has changed its worship practices many times during its long history. In the past, as recorded in the Jewish Scriptures, Jews worshiped by praying to God and by sacrificing animals, as other people did. The Exile brought about a major change in Jewish worship that continues to this day. Jews in exile in Babylon could not sacrifice, because they did not have access to the Jerusalem Temple, where all sacrifices had to take place. So, the Jewish people replaced sacrifice with prayer and the study of their Scriptures. Prayer became the central feature of Jewish worship.

The Jews during the Exile did not entirely invent this new form of universal Judaism. Ancient biblical prophets, such as Hosea and Isaiah, had emphasized that justice and mercy were more important than sacrifice. They taught that religion was largely a lifestyle of righteousness, demonstrated through acts of social justice. When the Romans destroyed the Jerusalem Temple in A.D. 70, the Jews never rebuilt it; they couldn't. They were kicked out of Jerusalem in 135 and never won back control of the city until 1967. By then, the Muslim holy site, the Dome of the Rock, stood on Temple Mount. Ever since the destruction of the Temple, Judaism has worshiped God without animal sacrifice or a central temple. Contemporary Jewish worship is held in a building known as a synagogue. In keeping with Judaism's emphasis on history, synagogue worship includes symbols and rituals that are designed to recall many ancient worship practices from the time of the Jerusalem Temple and the Exile.

THE SYNAGOGUE

This English name for the Jewish building of worship comes from the Greek word *synagogue*, which means "assembly." The Greek word *synagogue* is equivalent to the Hebrew *Bet Ha-Knesset*, which means "house of assembly." These Greek and Hebrew terms both refer to a place constructed especially for Jewish worship. The origins of the synagogue are found in the Exile, when the Jewish community prayed and studied the Tanakh in the absence of the Jerusalem Temple. Scribes, such as

Ezra and Nehemiah, became leaders of the community and publicly read the Scriptures to the Jewish people.

During the Exile, Aramaic replaced Hebrew as the dominant language in the Middle East. Portions of the Tanakh were even written in Aramaic. After a time, because many people no longer understood the Hebrew of the Tanakh, the Jewish priests would first read the Scriptures in Hebrew and then translate them into Aramaic, followed by some comments and explanations. This is the origin of the modern sermon, which seeks to explain and interpret scriptural texts. Today, as during the Exile, the Jewish synagogue is a place for prayer and study.

Scholars today disagree on the exact origin of the synagogue building. Some believe that the first synagogues were built in Babylon during the Exile. The earliest inscriptions and archaeological evidence of synagogue buildings date to the first century B.C., and come from Israel, Egypt, and Italy.

Early synagogue buildings were made of fine masonry, and contained an interior hall surrounded by benches. The benches were placed on all four sides of the building, so that the worshipers would face the center. Many ancient synagogues pointed toward Jerusalem, and contained decorations such as six-petaled rosettes flanked by date palms.

Synagogues also included a *mikveh*, a ritual purification bath, near their entrances. In antiquity, women traditionally immersed themselves in the mikveh before resuming sexual relations following their menstrual period. The waters of the mikveh symbolize purity. Converts to Judaism are still immersed in the mikveh today, as are couples before marriage. Some Jews today bathe in the mikveh on Fridays before Sabbath as well as on the day before Jewish holidays. A mikveh is normally located in a synagogue. More liberal Jewish synagogues do not often have a mikveh.

SYNAGOGUE DESIGN

There is no official design for the Jewish synagogue. Each of the subdivisions of Judaism has made some changes to the synagogue building. All contemporary Jewish synagogues descend from the design of the Orthodox synagogue, which is an adaptation of the ancient synagogue. The following description will focus on the design of the Orthodox synagogue, in order to illustrate the religious meaning of Jewish architecture, decoration, furnishings, and offices.

The interior of the synagogue is relatively simple and is largely designed to be functional. In antiquity, synagogues were built even though the Temple still existed in Jerusalem. After the destruction of the Temple, the synagogue underwent many changes. Many new structural elements were added to the building to remind Jews of the Jerusalem Temple, now entirely replaced by the synagogue. The ancient Jewish Temple in Jerusalem had been divided into three sections: an outer court for the people, where all Jews could pray; an inner sanctuary, open only to the priests, with an altar for sacrifice, a table for offerings, and a seven-branched candlestick that was always lit; and the Holy of Holies—the Temple's innermost room, which only the high priest could enter and only once each year, on the holiday of Yom Kippur. This room was empty, and represented the presence of God.

The modern Jewish synagogue generally follows the three-part pattern of the original Jerusalem Temple. The first section of the synagogue, the auditorium, corresponds to the ancient Temple's outer court. It is the place where the congregation sits during worship. The *Bimah*, or pulpit, represents the ancient Temple sanctuary, where the actual worship ceremonies took place. It is customary to have a light always on above the Bimah, to represent the eternal light that burned in the Jerusalem Temple. Today, it also symbolizes the concept that the light of the Torah will never be extinguished. The Holy Ark, which contains the Torah scrolls, corresponds to the ancient Temple's Holy of Holies.

Some traditional synagogues place a pitcher and washbasin by the synagogue entrance for people to wash their hands. This is done in order to fulfill the biblical commandment that one should approach the Temple with clean hands and a pure heart.

The synagogue is not a dark place. It must have windows like the ancient Temple. In the past, the synagogue was constructed at the highest place in a town. This is because the ancient Temple was located on a mountain and was visible throughout the city of Jerusalem. Today, many Jews have abandoned this custom; synagogues are now usually built in the most convenient location without regard to historic symbolism.

The Orthodox Jewish synagogue, frequently called a *shul*, is more than a building: It is the center of the Jewish community. Traditionally, a Jewish worship service cannot take place unless there is a quorum of ten men, called a *minyan*. More liberal forms of Judaism include women as part of the minyan. Orthodox Judaism, though, still follows tradition of only counts male Jews.

Orthodox Judaism divides the auditorium into separate

WHY DO SOME SYNAGOGUES CONTAIN A WOMEN'S GALLERY?

The origin of the women's gallery goes back to the ancient Jerusalem Temple, which contained a special court for women. When worshipers went to the Temple, they passed through a series of courts. Gentiles could worship in the outer areas of the Temple. Only Jews could pass through a wall that surrounded the Temple into the inner courts. Women were restricted to the first court. Men could go farther, but only priests could go near the Temple. Ancient synagogues, however, did not have a special area for women. Men and women sat together in the synagogue building.

The women's gallery is a relatively late development in Judaism. It was apparently created during the Rabbinical Era, and became widespread by the thirteenth century A.D. It seems to have been constructed for moral reasons; apparently, some Jewish holidays had become too festive and lasted late into the evening. The women's gallery was built to restrict contact between the sexes during certain Jewish festivities. It later became a permanent fixture in the synagogue. Over time, the original purpose of the women's gallery was lost and it became a means of limiting women's participation in worship services. Today, only Orthodox (and a few Conservative) synagogues contain a women's gallery.

sections for men and women. They are separated by a partition called a *mechitza*. (More liberal Jewish subdivisions of Judaism do not separate men from women. The presence of a separate seating area for women is a clear sign that a synagogue follows the traditions of Orthodox Judaism.) According to tradition, the mechitza should rise to three-quarters the height of the synagogue. The contemporary mechitza, however, varies in design and height. In many modern synagogues, it is actually a balcony. The separation of the sexes is mandatory in Orthodox synagogues. Except for prayer books (in Hebrew called *siddurim*) and Bibles (*chumashim*), all sacred objects in an Orthodox synagogue are located in the sections accessible only to men. Because women are only permitted to worship behind the mechitza, they do not have access to the other two sections of the synagogue.

SYNAGOGUE FURNISHINGS

The men's section makes up the main area of Orthodox synagogues. The most visible and prominent object is the Holy Ark (*Aron ha-Kodesh*), which holds the scrolls of the Torah. The Torah scroll is copied by a scribe on parchment. All the major subdivisions of Judaism have kept the tradition of using Torah scrolls during worship. The Torah scroll is considered sacred, and is believed to be able to sanctify anything with which it comes into contact. It is common for people to kiss the Torah, or touch it with the edge of a prayer cloak when it is paraded through the congregation during worship services. When the door of the Torah Ark is opened, the congregation rises to show respect. Many Jews believe that if a Torah scroll is dropped during worship, the entire congregation must fast for forty days.

The Torah is decorated with a breastplate, usually made of silver. The breastplate is attached to a chain and draped over the poles around which the Torah scroll is wrapped. These wooden poles are rolled as the Torah scroll is read. They are sometimes referred to as the "tree of life," a name that is sometimes used for the Torah as well. The breastplate that covers the Torah is designed to imitate the breastplate the high priest wore when he supervised worship in the ancient Jerusalem Temple. A crown is also placed on top of the Torah. According to one traditional story, this crown was added in accordance with a statement in an ancient Jewish book known as the *Pirke Avot*, or the *Ethics of the Fathers*. It proclaims: "There are three crowns: the crown of the Law (Torah), the crown of the Priestly office, and the crown of royalty, but the crown of a good name is above them all." Small bells are also placed on the Torah crown to represent the bells the high priest wore on his robe.

Other than the adornment on the Torah scrolls, Jewish synagogues usually have no decorations. This is in accordance with a strict interpretation of the Ten Commandments that prohibits the making of any graven image. Only decorations and art that are not three-dimensional are permitted. Depictions of the Ten Commandments are popular in synagogues. Many synagogues also contain a *menorah*. Originally a candlestick with seven branches, the menorah was the centerpiece of the Temple. Some Jews do not use a seven-branched menorah because it was used in the Temple; instead, they use a six-branched menorah. After the destruction of the Jewish Temple by the Romans in A.D. 70, some Jews felt that its furnishings should not be duplicated. The exact reason for this custom is unknown. An eight-branched menorah is used during the Jewish festival of Hanukkah. The six-pointed Star of David is another popular design in many synagogues. It is called the *Magen David* in Hebrew, which means "Shield of David." This design dates back over 1,800 years, and has become a common symbol of Judaism. The origin of the Star of David is unknown. Today, many Jews wear the Star of David as jewelry.

The Torah scroll is the most important object in the synagogue. It remains in the Ark behind doors and a curtain when it is not being used. In many synagogues, the doors are frequently decorated with lions, and tablets depicting the Ten Commandments. The curtain in front of the ark represents the portable tent shrine known as the Tabernacle. This structure was the Jewish place of sacrifice and worship from the time of Moses until the building of the first Jerusalem Temple around 950 B.C. All seats in the synagogue face the Torah shrine, which points east toward Jerusalem. In keeping with a custom recorded in the Tanakh, a portion of the Torah is read during worship. Originally, the prophet, priest, or king read the Torah. Over time, the honor of reading a passage from the Torah came to be divided among the male members of the congregation. Many Reform and some Conservative congregations now allow women to read from the Torah during worship, too.

SYNAGOGUE WORSHIP

Worship in the synagogue varies among the different subdivisions of Judaism. It usually follows a prayer book called a *Siddur*, which means "order." Holiday services follow a special prayer book called a *Machzor* ("cycle"). The prayer book contains both prayers and poems. Most of the prayers are in Hebrew, although some are in Aramaic, because this was one of the languages of ancient Judaism, as well as the language in which a few books in the Tanakh were originally written. Some more liberal forms of Judaism, such as the Reform movement, have translated most of the readings in their prayer books into English.

In some congregations, Jews sway when they pray. The origin of this physical movement, called *davening*, is uncertain. Some scholars believe it has its roots in practices done in the ancient Jerusalem Temple. Some prayers are recited while sitting, and others while standing.

Services are held three times a day in Orthodox synagogues, because this was the number of times daily that sacrifices were offered in the Jerusalem Temple. Weekly communal worship occurs in the Jewish synagogue on the Sabbath, the most holy day of the week. Sabbath worship is slightly different from daily worship, since the Sabbath is the highlight of the week, when the entire community assembles in the synagogue. The Jewish Sabbath begins at sunset on Friday night, and ends at sunset on Saturday night. This is because the ancient Jewish calendar marked the beginning of the day at nightfall. A special Friday night dinner typically precedes the Friday night synagogue service.

At Sabbath morning worship, seven people are usually called to read the Torah. (On Yom Kippur, six are called, and fewer on the other Jewish holidays.) The Torah follows a cycle of readings. It has become a tradition to read the entire Torah during the Sabbath services over the course of months or even years. In order to accomplish this, the Torah is divided into sections. In some traditions, the entire Torah is divided into 54 sections and is read in a single year. Other Jews divide the Torah into 155 portions, and read it over a period of three years. Reform and some Conservative congregations follow the three-year Torah reading cycle, while Orthodox and most Conservative Jews read the Torah in one year.

The honor of reading from the Torah is known as *aliya*, a Hebrew word that means "ascent." This term refers to the ascent that the reader makes when he or she steps onto the platform, or Bimah, to read. The Bimah is located in the middle of the synagogue, to show that the Torah is the center of the synagogue. In the Jerusalem Temple the altar was the focus of worship. Today, the Bimah has replaced the altar as the center of the community. In many Reform and Conservative synagogues, the Bimah is simply the space in front of the Torah, not a raised platform.

There are usually three *aliyot* (plural of *aliya*) during synagogue worship on the Sabbath afternoon. On major Jewish holidays such as Rosh Hashanah and Passover, there are five. There are six on Yom Kippur, and seven on Sabbath mornings. Some synagogues vary in the number of aliyot that occur during worship.

The person who is "called up" to read the Torah is known as an *oleh*. Although there are differences in the way the Torah is read in each subdivision of Judaism, the basic procedure is the same. The oleh is called by the synagogue official by his or her Hebrew name. A male oleh traditionally touches the Torah with the corner of his prayer shawl (*talit*) and kisses the torah at both the beginning and the end of the reading. Readers ascend the Bimah from the right, and depart from the left.

The oleh invites the congregation to praise God, and says, "Bless the Lord who is to be blessed." The congregation responds, "Blessed be the Lord, who is to be blessed for all eternity." Next, there is a blessing: "Blessed are You, Lord our

God, King of the universe, He, who has chosen us from among all the nations and given us His Torah. Blessed are You Lord, who gives the Torah." A portion of the Torah is then read. After the reading, the oleh says: "Blessed are You, Lord our God, Ruler of the universe, He who has given us a Torah of truth, thus implanting within us eternal life. Blessed are You, Lord, Giver of the Torah." The next oleh is then called to read. It is customary for the first oleh to remain on the Bimah until the next oleh has completed the second blessing. There are always at least three people on the Bimah whenever the Torah is read. This is to show that a person should not stand alone, because God gave the Torah to the Jews through intermediaries, the prophets.

Another person usually receives the honor of replacing the decorations on the Torah after it has been read. On Sabbaths and other festivals, a portion of the Haftarah, sections of the biblical books of the Prophets, is added to the reading. The worship service also includes a sermon, and readings from the prayer books.

Orthodox synagogues follow a traditional order for reading the Torah. Normally, the Torah is read publicly at the morning and afternoon services on each Sabbath. The first aliya is given to a *Kohayn*, and the second to a *Levite*. A Kohayn is a person who traces his ancestry to the ancient priests who supervised worship in the Jerusalem Temple. The Levites assisted the priests of the Temple. The remaining Jews, the Israelites (*Yisraelim*), traditionally read after the Kohayns and Levites. Reform Judaism no longer recognizes these ancient distinctions.

One person corrects any mistakes in the Torah reading. It is a custom to use a pointer called a *yad* (hand), usually made of silver, when reading from the Torah. The yad is a long stick that has a depiction of a hand with its index finger outstretched at the end. The Torah reader points to the words of the Torah with the yad as he reads. Because many Jews cannot read the Torah correctly in Hebrew, a professional Torah reader (*baal koray*) actually reads the Torah, and the person who received an aliya merely recites a blessing before and after the reading. Modern synagogues often have a baal koray today.

Modern synagogue worship varies among the different sub-divisions of Judaism. Each subdivision of Judaism has its own prayer books. Ashkenazic and Sephardic Jews pronounce the Hebrew and Aramaic languages differently. They also have different ways of printing certain Hebrew words in their prayer books. There are also differences in some of the prayers, which in Sephardic Judaism are frequently recited in unison, with a rhythmic cadence. Orthodox Judaism does not use instrumental music, while other branches may have lively songs performed by multiple instruments.

SYNAGOGUE OFFICES AND LITURGY

A person known as a rabbi typically leads the synagogue worship. In Judaism, a rabbi is not essential for the Sabbath service, however; any Jewish person can conduct worship. The rabbi is primarily a spiritual leader and teacher. Some congregations also have a person called a cantor (*chazzan*), who leads the congregation in prayer.

Worship traditionally is structured around two prayers: the *Shema* and the *Amidah*. The Shema is a declaration of belief in one God. The Amidah is a series of eighteen blessings. In order to fulfill the biblical commandment to wear God's blessings on the forehead, many Jews wear *tefillin* (phylacteries), which are small boxes containing verses of the Tanakh written by hand on parchment. These boxes are attached to straps. One strap is worn over the head, and the other is wound around the left arm, so that it is near the heart. The tefillin are worn during the morning synagogue service every day, except on the Sabbath and holidays. In Orthodox Judaism, only men wear the tefillin. Reform Judaism, however, allows women to wear them. A related object is the *mezuzah*. A mezuzah is a piece of parchment inscribed with verses from the Tanakh, rolled up and placed inside a small box that is nailed to a doorpost. This is a way to fulfill the commandment in the Torah to write the laws of God on the doorposts of houses and gates. Jews today place a mezuzah on the doorposts of their homes to remind them of God's laws.

The Amidah prayer is traditionally recited while standing. Jewish services normally include a prayer for the restoration of the Temple. In Reform Judaism, a prayer for the people is said instead, since a restoration of the Temple is not expected. The *Kaddish* and *Alenu* are two other important prayers. The Kaddish acknowledges God's sovereignty over the universe. It is said at the end of each major section of the liturgy, and by mourners at the end of the service. Jews are required to recite the Kaddish for eleven months after the death of a close relative. The Alenu prayer proclaims the kingship of God over the universe, and marks the conclusion of the service.

Men in Orthodox Judaism wear a prayer shawl called a *talit*, to remind them of God's laws. The prayer shawl is a very important part of Orthodox worship because of its historical significance. When the Jews of Sicily were expelled from their homes in 1493, they asked the authorities for permission to take their prayer shawls with them. During morning prayers, all males over the age of thirteen wear the talit. The corners of the talit contain fringes, which are reminiscent of the fringes worn by ancient Jews (Numbers 15:37–41). During synagogue services, men sometimes drape the talit over their heads before reciting prayers. Orthodox and some Conservative Jews believe that the talit must cover most of the body. In some synagogues, only married men wear the talit. In Orthodox and Conservative synagogues, worshipers are given a talit when they enter. Wearing a talit is optional in Reform Judaism.

In addition to the talit, many male Jews wear a prayer cap called a *yarmulke*, or *kippah*. The yarmulke goes back to the biblical command that the high priest cover his head (Exodus 28:4). It is believed that the yarmulke became common during the twelfth century A.D., when Christians demanded that Jews wear it in order to distinguish them from Christians.

Although the synagogue is important, the home remains the real focus of Judaism. The synagogue is an important institution, one that teaches children a great deal about religious practice. Still, many Jewish traditions and customs are learned at home during childhood.

6

Growing up Jewish

Train up a child in the way he should go,
Even when he is old he will not depart from it.

—Proverbs 22:6

Judaism has developed many rituals and traditions that regulate life from birth to death. When Jewish children are born, they immediately undergo ancient rituals designed to connect them with God and the Jewish community. Ritual ceremonies also mark the transition from childhood to adulthood, when the child officially becomes a member of the synagogue community. In the past, many of these rituals were restricted to men. Modern Jewish movements such as Reform and Conservative Judaism, though, have expanded some ancient Jewish rituals to include girls. Each of the different subdivisions of Judaism has its own traditions and ways for those growing up Jewish to practice the rituals.

CIRCUMCISION

In the Bible and ancient Jewish literature, sons were prized over daughters. In antiquity, men played the dominant social, economic, and religious roles. They were in charge of supporting the family and they controlled village life. For this reason, the first Jewish ritual—circumcision—is for males; it takes place eight days after birth. Circumcision is the surgical removal of the foreskin of the penis. According to the Tanakh, this ritual began in the time of Abraham. God ordered Abraham to circumcise all adult males as a sign of the covenant. All future sons were required to be circumcised eight days after they were born. In the past, the father of the child performed this operation, called the *brith milah*. Today, it is done by a professional called a *mohel*. A mohel does not have to be a rabbi or a physician. Any adult Jewish male may be trained as a mohel. In the past, a mohel did not receive any fee for his services, because circumcision was considered a divine commandment. Today, a mohel is paid; providing mohel services is often a full-time job.

Circumcision frequently takes place in the home. Parents appoint a *sandek* (godfather) to hold the child during the ceremony. Being selected to be a sandek is considered a great honor. A godmother is also chosen, to bring the child into the room for the ceremony. Guests are invited, and an elaborate meal is eaten following the ritual. An empty chair is usually placed in the room to represent the biblical prophet Elijah, whose eventual return was predicted by the prophet Micah. Because Elijah had denounced the Jewish people for not following the covenant strictly, Jewish tradition came to hold that Elijah attends every circumcision. The child to be circumcised is placed briefly in the Elijah chair before the ceremony. The child is then given a Hebrew name at the time he enters the covenant during the circumcision ritual. Circumcision remains an important Jewish ritual today for all Jews, because it symbolizes the covenant that God made with Abraham. It is a reminder that God is still with the Jewish people.

At the first Sabbath service after a baby's circumcision, the child's father is given a seat of honor and is called to read the Torah. For the birth of a daughter, a short blessing during the normal synagogue service is given. In recent times, there have been some attempts to create a special ceremony for baby girls. In Orthodox Judaism, a female child is given her name when the parents receive a blessing in the synagogue.

REDEMPTION OF THE FIRSTBORN

More traditional forms of Judaism still practice an ancient ceremony for males, known as *Pidyan Ha-Ben*. This ritual recalls the commandment God gave to Moses in the Book of Exodus to "consecrate to Me all firstborn: man and beast, the first issue of every womb among the Israelites is Mine." In antiquity, people believed that the gods were entitled to the first yield of the womb and the field. These were sacrificed to the gods. Judaism adopted this ancient custom for worship of the one God. In the Bible, Abraham was commanded to sacrifice his son Isaac. This was shocking, because Judaism does not permit murder, but it was, in fact, a test of Abraham's faith in God and the covenant. God intervened, stopping Abraham before Isaac was actually killed.

The Pidyan Ha-Ben ceremony takes place only if the newborn son is the firstborn male of his mother. Thirty days after birth, the child is ritually redeemed by the payment of a small sum of money to a priest. Today, in traditional forms of Judaism, people who trace their lineage to the ancient priests (*kohayns*), including people whose last name is Cohen, may receive this money. This is one of the few priestly roles that remain. Reform Judaism doubts the claims of priestly ancestry. Reform Judaism also does not recognize this ritual because it excludes girls.

EDUCATION

Judaism emphasizes education. According to ancient Jewish legal customs, parents have a duty to educate their children. Women have been traditionally exempt from most religious obligations, since their primary duty was to care for the children and home. For this reason, education was more important for males, since women did not wear the prayer shawl or other religious items nor were they required to attend regular prayer services at the synagogue. Women were largely educated apart from men and did not learn as much about the Bible or Talmud as young boys did. Traditionally, male and female children are treated similarly until they reach age three. In many communities, a boy's hair is not cut for the first three years. Some traditional forms of Judaism leave the side-curls hanging over the ears of males. Orthodox Jewish men wear these curls to fulfill the biblical commandment not to cut the corners of the hair. Once a young boy's hair is cut, he begins to learn verses from the Tanakh. Boys at this age start to wear the talit and a yarmulke on their heads to remind them of God's presence.

Although girls do not undergo any special rituals, they are treated as girls from age three: They are kept apart from men. More liberal forms of Judaism do not follow this traditional customs. In the past, most education occurred at home or in the village synagogue school. Today, young boys and girls attend schools that may be either public or religious. If they attend a public school, they usually attend special religious classes to learn about the different Jewish rituals and how to read Hebrew.

BAR MITZVAH

The *Bar Mitzvah* ("son of the commandment") is the traditional ceremony that marks the transition of a Jewish boy from youth to adulthood. It takes place when the boy is thirteen years old. From this point on, the boy is considered a man, responsible for his own conduct in religious matters.

The Bar Mitzvah ceremony became common during the fourteenth century. It is held in a synagogue, and the boy undergoing the ritual is called up to read the Torah. Boys usually go through special religious training to prepare them for the Bar Mitzvah ceremony. Because children do not participate in synagogue worship, the reading of the Torah in Hebrew is a public announcement that the boy is now an adult. Family and guests are invited to the ceremony. The completion of the Bar Mitzvah means that the child is now an adult for the purpose of fulfilling a *minyan*, which is the ten males required for a religious service to be held. A party frequently takes place at the conclusion of the Bar Mitzvah ceremony. At one time, Reform Judaism kept boys and girls in religious schools until age sixteen instead of holding the traditional Bar Mitzvah.

In traditional Judaism, a girl passed from youth to adulthood with no formal recognition. In recent times, some subdivisions of Judaism have conducted a ceremony for girls called a *Bat Mitzvah* ("daughter of the covenant"). The Bat Mitzvah is almost identical to the Bar Mitzvah. In Orthodox synagogues that recognize this ceremony, however, the girls do not read from the Torah. Reform and Conservative synagogues, on the other hand, may allow girls to read the Torah and play the same roles as males. The Bat Mitzvah takes place at age twelve.

ADULTHOOD

Adulthood in Judaism begins at age thirteen for males, and age twelve for girls. The age of adulthood is a year earlier for girls than for boys since Judaism recognizes that girls mature at a younger age than boys. From this point on, men and women are responsible for their own actions. They must follow the religious teachings of Judaism.

The most significant event of adulthood is marriage. Family has always been central to Judaism; celibacy is not considered a virtue. According to the Tanakh, the first humans, Adam and Eve, were told to procreate, as was Noah. Marriage in Judaism has traditionally been viewed as a legal transaction that gives a man exclusive rights over a woman.

In the past, marriages took place when the bride and groom were very young. Marriage brokers, called *shadkhan*, were dominant figures in Jewish life during the Middle Ages. This was because marriage was not merely a union of two individuals, but a joining of two families. Most liberal forms of Judaism have dispensed with the marriage broker, and allow people to choose their own spouses.

There are traditionally two components of a Jewish marriage ceremony. The first is the *erusin*, or *kiddushin*, which is a commitment before marriage that binds the couple together. It is almost like a real marriage, and requires a divorce to undo. The couple, however, does not yet live together.

The wedding day is a joyous time. It is preceded by the signing of a *ketubah*. The ketubah is a legal document that attests to the marriage. A ketubah is necessary for a Jewish marriage to occur. It is written in Aramaic, and records the legal obligations of the husband to the wife in the case of death or divorce. The obligations of the wife are traditionally not listed in the ketubah. Two witnesses sign the document. Because of its importance, the ketubah is frequently illustrated, and created to be a work of art. If a ketubah is lost, a new one must be made if the man and woman wish to continue to live together as husband and wife.

Traditional Jewish wedding ceremonies occur beneath a canopy called a *chupah*. A cantor frequently leads the prayers and sings at the wedding. Sometimes, the bride walks ritualistically around the groom either three or seven times. The origin of this custom is unknown. Some believe that it is an ancient belief that was intended to protect the husband from demons. The reason for the numbers three and seven is also unknown. The bride and groom drink from a glass of wine, and the groom places a ring on the bride's finger. He says, "Behold thou art betrothed to me with this ring in accordance with the Law of Moses and Israel." Next, seven benedictions are recited, during which the couple is blessed. The ceremony ends when the groom steps on a glass and breaks it. There are many theories about the origin of this custom; the most popular suggests that it is intended to remind Jews of the destruction of the Jerusalem Temple by the Romans in A.D. 70.

DEATH AND BURIAL

In Judaism, death is a time to honor the deceased. Jews have customarily forbidden artificial procedures to prolong life, because God is believed to be in control of everything. According to ancient Jewish tradition, a dying person was urged to make a final confession to God. The deathbed blessing, known as the Shema, says, "Hear O Israel, the Lord our God, the Lord is One." A dying person does not remain alone. Those present at the time of death usually rend their garments. All water in the vicinity is poured out of its containers because, according to tradition, it has been contaminated by the angel of death.

WHY DO JEWS PLACE A TOMBSTONE OVER A GRAVE?

Jews, like members of some other faiths, have always marked graves in order to remember the dead. There are several theories concerning the origin of this custom. According to some scholars, it goes back to the Tanakh, when Jacob set up a pillar to mark the grave of his wife, Rachel (Genesis 35:20). Marking a grave is considered a sign of respect. During the time when the Temple stood, tombstones also had another function: They marked areas that the priests should avoid. Cemeteries were considered impure, so priests avoided them in order to maintain state of ritual purity required to serve in the Temple. Some scholars believe that tombstones were erected in the Middle Ages by superstitious Jews who believed in ghosts. The tombstone kept the ghost of the deceased in the grave. It is common for many Jews today to leave a stone behind when visiting a grave to indicate that the deceased has not been forgotten. A large pile of stones atop a grave is a sign that the memory of the deceased is still kept alive by his or her family.

From Alfred J. Kolatch, *The Jewish Book of Why*. Middle Village, NY: Jonathan David, 1981, pp. 73–77.

Once someone dies, burial must take place as soon as possible—no more than two nights after the death. The body is washed and wrapped in white linen, and is then placed in a coffin that contains no metal. There are various types of funeral ceremonies for each of the subdivisions of Judaism. Orthodox Jews do not allow cremation, but Reform Judaism does.

At the funeral, a rabbi recites the *Kaddish*, an Aramaic prayer of praise for God and for peace. After the funeral, the family of the deceased returns home to sit *shiva*, observing a seven-day period of mourning. The focus after Jewish burial is largely upon the living. For one week, people come to visit the grieving family. The mourners recite the Kaddish three times each day to coincide with daily worship services. For the next thirty days, the Kaddish continues to be recited while the mourners return to normal life.

The dead person is remembered each year on the Hebrew date of his or her death. This anniversary is known as the *Yahrzeit*. It is celebrated by lighting a candle that burns for the entire day. This Jewish ritual is commonly observed by all subdivisions of Judaism, and by secular Jews, as a way to honor the dead.

The various rituals that surround death serve to bring the family together, to remind Jews of their past, and to help teach younger generations how to grow up Jewish.

EXPERIENCES OF GROWING UP JEWISH

Just as there are many different ways to practice Judaism, there are many different ways to grow up Jewish. Sometimes even Jews who live in close proximity to one another are raised in religious traditions that have little in common with one another. Contemporary Jewish novelist Chaim Potok's novel *The Chosen* examines the problems that may occur when different types of Judaism exist in the same city. His book, set against the backdrop of World War II, focuses on two young boys, Reuven and Danny, who were raised in religious traditions that were alien to each other. Reuven was raised in a yeshiva, a religious school, at which his father was a teacher. Danny was brought up in a small Hasidic yeshiva established by his father. Unlike Danny, Reuven was raised to practice a liberal form of Judaism. Conservative Jews looked down upon his yeshiva because it offered more English subjects and was not considered as religious as the other Jewish schools. Although the two boys were both young Jews, Reuven and Danny at first found the other types of Judaism in their neighborhood foreign and unlike the faith each learned at home. The boys had little in common, and it seemed unlikely that they would become friends. Over time, however, they learned to appreciate the different types of Judaism. Such is the situation in modern Judaism. Not only is the story of growing up Jewish different from country to country, but sometimes, as Chaim Potok's novel accurately demonstrates, from neighborhood to neighborhood. Every Jewish person has his or her own unique story about growing up Jewish.

The writer Elie Wiesel, winner of the 1986 Nobel Peace Prize, has written extensively about growing up Jewish in Hungary during World War II. Raised in a traditional Jewish family, in which no decisions were made unless the rabbi was consulted, Wiesel later had a crisis of faith. His town of Sighet was so religious that people used to joke that everyone, even atheists, had their own synagogue. Religion dominated all facets of life: It gave people a feeling of peace and security. Wiesel writes that, as a child, he often accompanied his mother to visit the rabbi, who would bless him. When the war broke out, Elie Wiesel was deported to the concentration camp of Auschwitz and then to Buchenwald, where his parents and young sister died. Commenting on this experience, Wiesel wrote: "The war turned everything upside down, changing the order and substance of priorities. For me, to be a Jew today means telling the story of this change." Wiesel later became a university professor and has spent the rest of his life telling the story of the Holocaust and writing about the Jewish culture in which he grew up. Although the Judaism of his native land no longer exists because of the tragic events of the Holocaust, Wiesel strives to keep alive the traditions of his homeland by continuing to tell his story. Preserving the story of the Jewish people is central to Wiesel's life and keeps him connected to his ancient religious heritage, which has always emphasized story.

Story has always been a key part of the Jewish tradition. For many Jews who lived during World War II, survival was the primary issue. Some of these Jews, like Elie Wiesel, have dedicated their lives to telling the story of their suffering and other tales about the remarkable survival of the Jewish people. The story of Anne Frank is one of the most memorable tales to emerge from the Holocaust. Growing up in Amsterdam, Anne Frank, along with her parents, sister, and several other Jews, hid in an attic for two years during the Nazi occupation of Holland. From the time she was thirteen until she was fifteen, Anne lived in constant fear and isolation from the surrounding world, unable to make a sound or move during the day. In August 1944, the Nazis discovered the Franks' hiding place: Someone had betrayed the family. Everyone in the attic was taken away by the Nazis. Anne later perished in a concentration camp.

During her confinement in the attic, Anne kept a diary in which she told the story of her suffering and her thoughts about growing up. Her diary was later discovered and was published after the war. It remains one of the classic stories about growing up Jewish during World War II. Although Anne Frank and Elie Wiesel had very different experiences growing up Jewish during World War II, they both shared an interest in telling their stories.

Other Jewish writers have followed their lead. Phyllis Grodsky writes about growing up Jewish in the late 1940s in the South Bronx of New York City. Her experience, although contemporary with those of Elie Wiesel and Anne Frank, was very different. She did not have to be afraid to practice her religion. Grodsky, however, was not able to have a Bat Mitzvah, since the Orthodox Judaism in which she was raised does not recognize this ceremony. Consequently, she sometimes felt left out of Judaism's rituals and showed little interest in learning about them. Her father somehow arranged for her to attend Hebrew school, which was normally restricted to boys at that time. Grodsky, however, never connected to the traditions of Orthodox Judaism. Although her father was deeply religious, she often found Orthodox Judaism foreign and strange because it did not permit women to celebrate the same religious rituals as boys. Despite her father's lifestyle and observance, Grodsky still did not feel at home within Orthodox Judaism. Even as she learned the traditional prayers alongside boys in Hebrew school, she could not connect. She lost interest in the classes and stopped attending Hebrew school. Even so, the Jewish education she received has remained with her to the present day as she continues to share her stories about growing up Jewish. Though Grodsky no longer practices the Judaism of her youth, she, like many other Jews who have changed their understanding of their religion, still remain part of the Jewish tradition. Telling her story, like many other Jews, is a vital component of her religious heritage.

Edward Cohen shares yet another experience, that of growing up Jewish in Jackson, Mississippi, during the 1950s. According to Cohen, it was a very difficult experience. His hometown was in the heart of the so-called Bible Belt, a region dominated by conservative Christianity. Cohen's grandfather had left Romania and moved to Mississippi, where he worked as a peddler. For most people, he was the first Jew they had ever seen. Cohen grew up among his Jewish extended family of cousins, isolated from outsiders, until he began to attend school. He soon realized that he was the only Jew in his class. While the other students looked forward to Christmas, Cohen celebrated Rosh Hashanah. He quickly learned that he had very little in common with most of the other children.

Although Jews were viewed as different from other citizens, his town nonetheless granted them more rights than African

Americans had. As he grew up, Cohen learned to appreciate the similarities between his Jewish culture and the South: Both had a long and tragic history. African Americans, and to some extent, Jews, were not full citizens. Today, Edward Cohen continues to tell the story of how the Jews in his town managed to preserve their faith as a religious minority in a region dominated by Christianity and racial segregation. His story preserves the memory of this bygone era when people were less tolerant of those who came from different religious traditions or races.

These stories are just few examples of the many different ways that Jews have grown up and learned their religion's traditions. For most Jews, the central issue in growing up Jewish is learning to live as a minority among people who practice another religion. In many instances, such as in Cohen's story and Chaim Potok's novel, Jews live in close proximity to one another, which helps them carry on their traditions. Sometimes, as Edward Cohen describes, young Jewish children live in an entirely Jewish environment until they are old enough to attend school. It is during the school years that many Jews first learn how different they are from their neighbors, most of whom practice Christianity. In some instances they are accepted, but in many places, they may be looked upon with suspicion. Today, however, the situation is rapidly changing. As the United States and Europe continue to absorb immigrants from all around the world, people are becoming more accustomed to living beside those who belong to other races or religions. The experience of today's young Jews will undoubtedly be vastly different from that of their parents and grandparents.

7

Cultural
Expressions

Hear, O Israel! The Lord our God, the Lord is One.
And thou shalt love the Lord thy God, with all thy heart,
and with all thy soul, and with all thy might.
And these words which I command thee this day
shall be in thy heart. And thou shalt teach
diligently unto thy children. . . .

—Deuteronomy 6:4–7

FROM THE
JEWISH
TRADITION

God the Father. It is rare for Jewish houses of worship to contain depictions of God, since Judaism tends to define such works as idolatry. Because both Judaism and Christianity worship the same God, however, representations of God—often referred to by Jews as "Adonai"—can be found in Christian churches. This stained glass from the tympanum of a window in the Cathedral of Rouen in France is an image of God the Father. It was created during the sixteenth century, probably around 1530.

The Sacrifice of Isaac. Abraham's obedience to God when commanded to sacrifice his son Isaac is a theme that resonates through both Jewish and Christian beliefs. Because the biblical story, in which God sends an angel to stop the sacrifice just in time to save Isaac, is so well known, it has often been the subject of works of art by famous painters. This representation of the event was painted by Renaissance-era Italian artist Michelangelo Merisi da Caravaggio. Believed to have been completed in 1603 or 1604, the work shows an angel (at far left), grabbing Abraham's arm to stop him from slitting Isaac's throat.

Moses Leading the Children of Israel. The artist who created this piece, which depicts Moses leading the children of Israel through the Red Sea, was Nicolas of Verdun. Despite the many artworks attributed to him, the details of Nicolas of Verdun's life are little known. He is believed to have been born around 1150 and died around 1205. Many historians believe that Nicolas was equally skilled in four trades: goldsmith, painter, sculptor, and enamel expert. He is most famous for his panels, like this one, completed around 1181, that graces the altarpiece at Klosterneuburg Abbey in Austria. Art historians say that the main goal of Nicolas's works was to help people better understand their role within God's plan for both heaven and Earth.

Abraham Representing Paradise. In this page from a prayer missal, created sometime between 1200 and 1232, Abraham serves as a representation of the paradise that awaits the righteous after they die. Depicted with a halo that signifies his holiness, Abraham sits on a throne and gathers to him the good people who are being called to heaven. This piece of art, now stored in the Pierpont Morgan Library in New York, originally comes from the Abbey of Weingarten in Germany.

Ruins of the Synagogue in Bar'am. Bar'am was an ancient Jewish village located in Upper Galilee. The synagogue's ruins were excavated in the twentieth century. This synagogue, built there in the fifth century, faced south, toward Jerusalem. The large building is architecturally similar to other synagogues of the Talmudic period, but it does have one unique feature: the enormous six-column portico that runs the entire length of the façade. Some historians claim Bar'am was chosen as the site for this synagogue because it was believed to have been the burial place of Queen Esther.

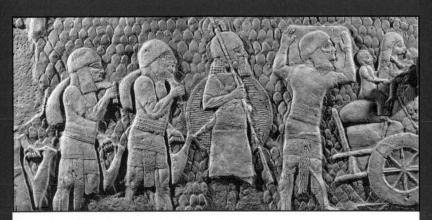

Jewish Exiles. This relief sculpture, done in the eighth century B.C., depicts Jewish exiles carrying provisions as they leave their homeland after the Assyrian conquest of the town of Lachish in 701 B.C. The piece, whose sculptor is unknown, was originally found at the palace of Sennacherib in Nineveh, an ancient city located in what is now Iraq on the banks of the Tigris River. Most likely the work of an Assyrian artist, the scene represents the Assyrians' victory over the Jews.

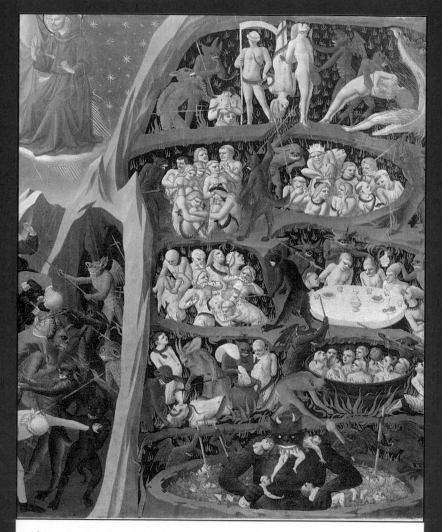

Sinners Facing Torment in Hell. Originally, Judaism held no belief in an afterlife in which people would be punished or rewarded for their deeds on Earth. During the time of the Exile, the concepts of heaven, hell, and resurrection developed, perhaps as a way to reassure the Jews that they would be compensated after death for the suffering they were facing during life. This detail from Christian artist Fra Angelico's painting *Last Judgment*, created between 1432 and 1435, depicts sinners undergoing terrible torment in hell.

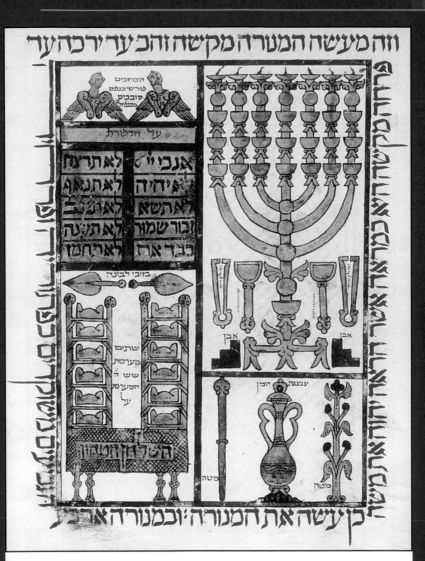

Jewish Ritual Objects. This page from an illuminated manuscript was created around 1300. It depicts a series of Jewish ritual objects, many of which are still used today. For example, at the top right of the page is the traditional seven-branched candlestick that was always kept lit to remind Jews of God's constant presence. Below that is a kadisha vessel, which is used by the Chevra Kadisha, the group of people who bear responsibility for ensuring the proper burial of Jews.

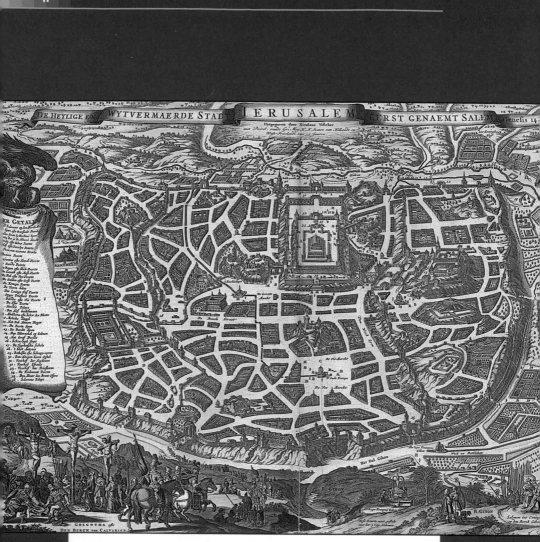

The City of Jerusalem. This map of the city of Jerusalem was designed by Dutch artist Nicolaes Visscher during the mid-seventeenth century. Originally intended to be published within an edition of the Bible, it was instead bound on its own. The major buildings and other sites are numbered and identified in the key at left (in Dutch). The map also depicts scenes from Judeo-Christian history. At bottom right, for example, Solomon is being crowned king of the Jews.

Because Judaism has existed for thousands of years, it has developed a distinctive culture. Judaism's contributions to contemporary American and world cultures are immense. Western civilization, for example, has essentially adopted the Jewish ethical system, as found in the Tanakh. Christians still emphasize adherence to the Ten Commandments given to Moses. The common culture of the Western world is frequently referred to as "Judeo-Christian," acknowledging the influences of both Judaism and Christianity. Because Christianity emerged from Judaism, Western civilization is, to a great extent, a legacy of Judaism.

Jews have not only made many contributions to Western civilization; they have also greatly enhanced Islamic culture. Especially during the periods when they lived under Islamic rule, Jews made many significant advances in medicine. Because Muslims were tolerant of Judaism, Jewish culture thrived under Islamic rule. The Talmud, for example, was written in Babylon and still forms the basis for Orthodox Judaism. Jewish literary and theological writing flourished under the rule of the Muslims. The Koran (Qur'an), the sacred scripture of Islam, contains many stories that come from the Jewish Tanakh. For this reason, Middle Eastern and other countries dominated by Islam continue to be influenced by the cultural legacy of Judaism.

Judaism has experienced many centuries of persecution and anti-Semitism. Because Jews have always been a minority community, they have seldom been able to physically resist persecution. They have tried to live peacefully with their neighbors as best they could.

Different aspects of Jewish culture have helped Jews survive as a people. For example, Judaism has developed a unique sense of humor to deal with suffering. Story-telling is also important, especially in Hasidic Judaism. In the past, Judaism obeyed a strict interpretation of the Ten Commandments that forbade the making of graven images. Jewish art tended to be restricted to the decoration of manuscripts and synagogues. In more recent times, however, Jewish artists have abandoned this literal interpretation and have entered the world of art. Jews have also developed distinctive forms of music. Contemporary American culture continues to be heavily influenced by Jewish literature, music, and humor—although many people do not realize that some forms of entertainment have Jewish origins.

CONTRIBUTIONS OF JEWS TO AMERICAN CULTURE

Jews have made significant contributions to American society throughout U.S. history. Some scholars believe that a few Jews even sailed with Christopher Columbus and helped discover the New World. The first Jews to settle in America were of Sephardic and Ashkenazic origin. They arrived in the Dutch settlement of New Amsterdam (later known as the city of New York) in 1654. The Dutch had settled in Brazil during the seventeenth century, but were forced to leave when the Portuguese took control of Brazil in 1654. At this time, a group of Jews moved from Brazil to New Amsterdam. Peter Stuyvesant, the leader of New Amsterdam, did not welcome them. The Jewish settlers were not permitted to build a synagogue. Some colonists, however, gave the Jews better treatment. In 1664, when the British took over New Amsterdam, the situation changed. The first Jewish congregation, named Shearith Israel, was organized around 1706. About 1730, a small synagogue was constructed. Jewish communities spread throughout the early American colonies and have continued to enrich American culture ever since. Today, the Touro Synagogue of Newport, Rhode Island, dedicated in 1763, is the oldest extant synagogue building in North America.

Jews have participated in all aspects of American society since the creation of the United States and even before. Jews fought during the American Revolution and served under George Washington. A Jew named Samuel Sanders accompanied Daniel Boone on his explorations, and was present at the siege of Boonesborough. Lewis Adler and Jacob Frankfort were among the first California settlers. Jacob Hirschorn became a hero in the Mexican War of 1846–1848. Jews served on both sides in the

American Civil War (1861–1865). Because Jews have played an instrumental role in building the United States, their legacy lives on in American history and contemporary culture.

JEWISH CULTURAL CONTRIBUTIONS

Jews lived as a minority in their countries until the creation of the modern state of Israel. Despite their small numbers, Jews contributed significantly to world culture. Jews have been leaders in many fields. The Jewish teacher and philosopher Martin Buber (1878–1965), in his book *I and Thou*, taught that every "I" and "Thou" relationship in the world is an encounter with the divine. Buber stressed the sacredness of everyday relationships; his ideas continue to influence modern psychology and social thought.

In fact, Jews have had a major effect in the field of mental health and, to a large extent, they helped invent modern psychology. Sigmund Freud (1856–1939), the Jewish founder of psychoanalysis, was forced to flee his home in Austria to escape the Nazis. His study of dreams and the unconscious mind formed the basis for many modern psychological treatments. Abraham Maslow (1908–1970) and Viktor Frankl (1905–1997) added religious dimensions to psychology. Unlike Freud, Maslow and Frankl believed that religion was essential for meaning, and they brought religious themes—shaped by their Jewish upbringings—into their works.

Jews have made many contributions to music, art, and literature. Ernest Bloch (1880–1959) wrote musical works that were inspired by Jewish liturgical melodies, such as those from the Yom Kippur service. The famed conductor Leonard Bernstein (1918–1990) wrote several works with Jewish themes. He is perhaps best known for his musical *West Side Story*, which continues to be popular today. The Jewish bandleader Benny Goodman was also one of the most famous American musicians. Marc Chagall (1887–1985) is perhaps the most renowned Jewish artist. His works frequently incorporated themes from the Jewish world of his Russian homeland.

Jews were also pioneers in the film industry. They entered the field during its early years, since film was not considered a violation of the traditional Jewish prohibition against making graven images. Because it was a new industry, Jews in the movie business did not face discrimination in this profession at a time when they were still restricted from holding many types of jobs in American society. In the United States, Ashkenazic Jews largely created the media industry, and Jewish themes were frequently seen in their works. The first major American film, *The Jazz Singer*, released in 1927, is about a Jewish man who wants to become a popular singer. It featured the Jewish actor and vocalist Al Jolson. This movie was so popular that it was remade in a 1980 version that starred pop singer Neil Diamond. In 1983, the contemporary Jewish singer Barbara Streisand also made a Jewish film, *Yentl*, which dealt with the theme of gender equality. Films such as *Sophie's Choice* (1982) and *Schindler's List* (1993) examined the Holocaust, in order to educate the public about the consequences of anti-Semitism. Jewish screenwriters and filmmakers still hold a dominant place in the Hollywood movie industry because they were there from its beginnings.

In literature, contemporary authors such as Saul Bellow, Elie Wiesel, and Chaim Potok have influenced modern culture through their novels and works that contain Jewish themes. Elie Wiesel's novel, *Night*, based on his experiences during the Holocaust, has educated a new generation of non-Jews about the tragic history of anti-Semitism. There are too many influential Jewish authors and screenwriters to name; just a few of the most famous include Isaac Asimov, Marcel Proust, Allen Ginsberg, Danielle Steel, Carl Sagan, J.D. Salinger, Naomi Wolf, and Dorothy Parker. This list could be expanded to include many more Jews who have enriched contemporary American and world culture.

JUDAISM IN AMERICAN POPULAR CULTURE

Considering Judaism's contributions to American society, it is not surprising that it continues to play a major role in popular culture. Many American television shows feature Jewish themes. Jewish comedian Jerry Seinfeld's television show, *Seinfeld*, incorporated numerous Jewish topics. Episodes dealt with circumcision and interfaith marriage, and included a character who was a rabbi. Yiddish words such as *shlemiel* and *shlemozzel*, both of which describe funny characters, became household terms thanks to their use in the popular 1970s television series *Laverne and Shirley*. Pop icon Madonna has studied the teachings of the Kabbalah, and incorporates them into her music and videos.

The teachings of the Kabbalah continue to attract Hollywood celebrities. Many of these stars merge the beliefs of the Jewish mystical tradition with the teachings and practices of New Age religions. The term "New Age" is difficult to define, since adherents of New Age spirituality follow many diverse teachings. New Age religions generally teach that personally transformed individuals will eventually change the planet. Not confining themselves to a single religious tradition, followers of New Age spirituality frequently merge teachings from a variety of indigenous religions and Asian faiths alongside Western beliefs in order to transform themselves spiritually. Many have subsequently merged the teachings of the Kabbalah into their New Age religion because of its similarities with the traditions of indigenous and Asian religions, which stress divine mystery.

In the West, some New Age practitioners have combined teachings of Native American religions, Christianity, and the Kabbalah to emphasize union with God. Common techniques to accomplish this include meditation, breathing exercises, ritualistic dancing, and yoga. These practices, according to many New Age followers, will help people attain a mystical union with God, which is the goal of Jews who follow the teachings of the Kabbalah. Today, many people are becoming acquainted with the teachings of the Kabbalah through New Age forms and the testimonies of its celebrity followers, inlcuding Madonna, Elizabeth Taylor, Goldie Hawn, and Demi Moore. Most Jews who follow the teachings of the Kabbalah do not consider these New Age versions of their religion valid, since the Kabbalah emphasizes that the spiritual quest requires a lifetime of prayer and study. In contrast to the traditional practices of the Kabbalah, New Age versions often teach that mysticism and a union with God are easily obtainable and do not require in-depth learning in Jewish culture, tradition, and literature.

Other aspects of American society have affected Jewish practices. The feminist movement has strongly influenced contemporary Judaism. Many Jewish women reject traditional forms of Judaism that restrict religious roles to men, and have either joined one of the more liberal subdivisions of Judaism, or formed their own religious communities. An increasing number of women belong to Jewish groups that count them as part of a minyan. They also seek to focus on the study of biblical women, such as Miriam and Huldah, who were prophetesses in the

A Jewish Pirate

During the nineteenth century, bands of pirates terrorized the coasts of America. Able to hide in swampy coves and inlets, they frequently pillaged and plundered American, British, and Spanish ships. Among the most famous of these raiders was the Jewish pirate Jean Lafitte, known as a pirate chief. Lafitte and his band of pirates, including his brothers, controlled the territory around New Orleans, Louisiana. When the British asked Lafitte to guide them through the swamps to attack the Americans, Lafitte warned the Americans of the impending British attack on New Orleans. Lafitte and his men assisted General Andrew Jackson, who later became president of the United States, by guiding his men through the marshlands and guarding the fort at Lake Pontchartrain. With Lafitte's help, the Americans were able to defend New Orleans against the British. Some Jewish residents of the city even participated in the battle. To thank Lafitte for his services in helping the United States, President James Madison issued a presidential pardon on February 6, 1815, to the pirate chief and his band of buccaneers. Many of Lafitte's men subsequently gave up the pirate life and earned their living as fishermen.

For more information on Jean Laffite and other Jewish pirates, see Harold Sharfman, *The Frontier Jews: An Account of Jewish Pioneers and Settlers in Early America.* Secaucus, NJ: The Citadel Press, 1978.

Tanakh. The Jewish feminist scholar Susannah Heschel points to women-related themes in Jewish literature, and encourages the use of language for naming God that is neither masculine or feminine.

In recent times, Judaism has become more accepted by non-Jewish Americans. When anti-Semitism does occur, Jews have recourse to the U.S. legal system for protection. The 2000 presidential election exemplified how much Judaism has become an integrated part of American society. Jewish politician Joseph Lieberman came close to becoming the vice president of the United States when he ran on the Democratic ticket with Al Gore. Lieberman frequently speaks about the importance of his faith as an observant Jew, and Judaism's emphasis upon ethics as the basis for his public service. Lieberman demonstrates that it is possible to practice traditional forms of Judaism while fully participating in, and making significant contributions to, contemporary American culture.

8

Holidays

*You shall also observe the Feast of Unleavened Bread,
for on this very day I brought your hosts out of the land
of Egypt; therefore you shall observe this day throughout
your generations as a permanent ordinance.*

—Exodus 12:17

Judaism is a festive religion, with many holidays that commemorate significant events in Jewish history. The Jewish Sabbath is also considered a holy and festive day that reminds Jews of their history and connection with God. Most contemporary Jewish holidays began in the biblical period, and are documented in the Tanakh. Over time, these biblical festivals and holy days were updated to reflect changing times. The holiday of Hanukkah, for example, was added after the biblical period to commemorate the Jewish victory in 165 B.C. over the Syrian Greeks, who had attempted to eradicate the Jewish religion. Despite their diversity, all of the Jewish holidays are in some manner tied to history. They bring the community together to remind Jews of God's past actions on behalf of the Jewish people. As commemorations of these acts of God, Jewish holidays are very important and remain a central part of the Jewish lifestyle.

THE CALENDAR

The Jewish calendar is lunar, and contains twelve months. There are 354 days in a lunar year. Months begin with the new moon and last either 29 or 30 days. Because the Jewish calendar is lunar, unlike with the modern solar calendar of 365 days, Jewish holidays do not occur on the same date each year. Every month in the Jewish calendar begins on the new moon, which is the time when the first sliver of the moon is visible after the dark of the moon. The problem with this calendar is that there are approximately 12.4 lunar months in the solar year. This means that the twelve-month lunar calendar loses about eleven days each year. For example, the month of Nissan, which is supposed to occur in the spring, drifts back eleven days earlier each year until it occurs in winter, fall, summer, and then spring again. In order to avoid these shifts, an extra month is occasionally added to the calendar. The rabbi Hillel II made adjustments to the Jewish lunar calendar in the fourth century A.D. to fix the dates of the festivals.

The calendar used in most Western countries actually counts its years based on the traditional date on which Jews believed the world was created. Based on the time difference between the two calendars, our year A.D. 2000 was the year 5760 on the Jewish calendar.

Today, there is a debate in Judaism over the calendar. The Tanakh prescribes one-day festivals. This direction is followed by Jews in Israel. Orthodox Judaism sets aside two days for all holy days for Diaspora Jews. Reform Judaism does not follow two-day celebrations, while Conservative Judaism allows rabbis the option of observing one- or two-day festivals. The custom of celebrating festivals for two days is not in the Bible, but emerged because Jews in the past could not always determine when the new moon appeared, which marked the beginning of each month. The rabbis decreed that festivals would be celebrated for two days since many calendars (because the new moon was not visible in the sky) were sometimes off by one day until word reached villages regarding the correct date. Reform Jews have abandoned this custom, which they no longer consider relevant.

SABBATH *(SHABBAT)*

The Sabbath is the most important of all Jewish holidays. It fulfills God's command in the Tanakh that humans should relax on the seventh day of the week. The Sabbath begins every Friday at sundown, and ends at sundown on Saturday. There are many different ways to celebrate the Sabbath, and each of the different subdivisions of Judaism has its own rituals. A special meal is usually eaten, traditionally the best meal of the week. During the meal, the Kiddush, a benediction over wine and bread, is recited. Candles are lit and blessed by the woman of the house.

Conservative and Orthodox Jews hold synagogue services on Saturday morning, when they read that week's section of the Torah. In some conservative forms of Judaism, it is customary to read the Torah every Sabbath at morning and afternoon services.

The Sabbath is a joyous time when friends and family gather together to study the Torah and worship God.

Orthodox Judaism today still follows biblical restrictions against lighting or extinguishing fires and lights, smoking, carrying money, or performing labor on the Sabbath. More liberal Jews no longer adhere to these Sabbath restrictions.

PASSOVER (*PESACH*)

Passover (*Pesach*) commemorates the time during the Exodus when the angel of death passed over the Israelites. It is one of the three pilgrim festivals mentioned in the biblical Book of Deuteronomy, along with *Shavuot* and *Sukkoth*, when all males were required to appear before God. When the Jerusalem Temple stood, Jews went there to celebrate these three festivals.

The festivals were designed to commemorate acts of God, but they also have agricultural connotations. Passover marks not only the Exodus, but also the beginning of the barley harvest. It lasts for seven days in Israel, and eight days outside of Israel. Jews must not eat any bread made with leavening agents or yeast during Passover. A special meal, called a *seder*, is eaten. During the Exodus, God commanded the Israelites to eat a meal of roasted lamb, unleavened bread, and bitter herbs. The bitter herbs symbolized their bondage in Egypt. The unleavened bread was eaten because the Israelites did not have time to bake bread with yeast. Seder reminds Jews of the Exodus, when God delivered the Jewish people from slavery in Egypt. When Jews gather together each year to partake of this meal, they are symbolically reliving the events of the Exodus and remembering God's deliverance of the Jewish people. Passover is different from other Jewish holidays, because its highpoint takes place in the home, at a meal, rather than in the formal setting of the synagogue. Over time, other items were added to this meal to commemorate the Exodus. Salt represents tears, and horseradish depicts the bitterness of slavery. Wine reminds Jews that they are now free. Eggs and fresh greens represent the hope of spring, and rebirth.

THE FEAST OF WEEKS (*SHAVUOT*)

The Feast of Weeks, or *Shavuot*, takes place fifty days after Passover. It commemorates the day that Moses received the Torah from God on Mount Sinai. Shavuot is called Pentecost in the Christian New Testament. It was originally a festival to celebrate the first grain harvest, and was later connected to the Exodus event. During Shavuot, Jews eat dairy foods to symbolize that the Torah, like milk, nourishes everyone from youth to old age. Shavuot is the time when boys and girls traditionally graduate from Hebrew school.

NEW YEAR (*ROSH HASHANAH*)

Rosh Hashanah (New Year's Day) is celebrated at the beginning of the traditional Jewish calendar. It marks a ten-day period of penitence that concludes with the Day of Atonement (*Yom Kippur*). According to the Jewish text known as the *Mishnah*, humans pass before God at the New Year and are subject to judgment. Some are judged to be righteous, and some are deemed wicked. Most people are somewhere in between, and must repent for their evil deeds during the ten days before Yom Kippur. On Rosh Hashanah, a ram's horn, called a *shofar*, is blown, to call people to repentance.

THE DAY OF ATONEMENT (*YOM KIPPUR*)

Yom Kippur is the most sacred day of the Jewish year. All adult Jews are expected to fast from sunset until nightfall the next day, to atone for their sins. Jews spend the Day of Atonement in the synagogue. During the Yom Kippur service, the congregation chants a prayer known as *Kol Nidre*, which asks God's forgiveness for sin and for any unfulfilled vows made in the Lord's name.

Some Jews observe another fast day, *Tisha B'Av*. This fast takes place on the ninth day of the month of Av (the fifth month of the Jewish year), to commemorate the destruction of the Jerusalem Temple by both the Babylonians in 586/587 B.C.

and the Romans in A.D. 70. According to Jewish tradition, the Temple was destroyed twice on this same day. Reform congregations do not generally celebrate this holiday, because they do not expect the Temple to be rebuilt.

THE FEAST OF TABERNACLES (*SUKKOTH*)

Sukkoth is a harvest festival that takes place five days after Yom Kippur. Over time this autumn festival became attached to the Exodus. It now commemorates the time when the Jews wandered in the Sinai Desert on their way to Israel. During the time of wandering, the Israelites lived in booths, or tabernacles, called *sukkoth* (the singular is *sukkah*). Jews build booths and sit in them during the festival to recall the Exodus experience. Jews in Israel live in these booths for eight days, and Jews outside of Israel for nine days.

Jews also make a *lulav*, which is a bundle of palm, willow, and myrtle branches. They wave the lulav and an *etrog*, a lemon-like fruit sometimes called a citron, in all directions in the synagogue, to symbolize God's control of everything. The final day of this religious holiday is known as *Simhat Torah* ("Joy in Torah"). In traditional Judaism, a portion of the Torah is read during each synagogue service. Simhat Torah marks the end of the yearly cycle of Torah readings.

THE FEAST OF DEDICATION (*HANUKKAH*)

Hanukkah, also known as the Feast of Dedication or the Feast (or Festival) of Lights, celebrates the deliverance of the Jews from the Syrian Greeks. In 165 B.C., the Jewish leader Judas Maccabaeus fought the Syrian Greeks who had attempted to destroy Judaism. Judas and his family fought a guerrilla war to reclaim the Jerusalem Temple. According to one tradition, when the Jews recaptured the Temple, there was only a single container of oil to light the lamps. Although the oil should have lasted for just one night, it lasted for eight days, which was the time the Jews needed to make new oil. To commemorate this event, Jews light candles for eight days.

Traditionally, Hanukkah has been a minor holiday, because it is not mentioned in the Tanakh. It has recently increased in importance among Jews in the United States, though, since it occurs near Christmas. Perhaps because of the appeal of gift-giving, Hanukkah has evolved to be a counterpart to Christmas.

THE FEAST OF LOTS (*PURIM*)

Purim commemorates events recorded in the biblical Book of Esther. In the Tanakh, Esther, a Jewess, was the wife of the king of Persia. When she learned of a plot led by the king's wicked advisor, Haman, to destroy the Jews in that country, she intervened to save her people. Lots were cast to determine which day the Jews would be destroyed. The festival is known as *Purim*, which means "lots," to commemorate this event. On Purim, the Book of Esther is read in synagogue. It is a joyful holiday, and gifts are exchanged.

Judaism is a religion dominated by history and memory. All the holidays and festivals of Judaism are in some manner connected with events in the Jewish past, in keeping with Judaism's focus on history. In order to understand contemporary Judaism, it is essential to learn something about the importance of Jewish memories.

PERSONAL EXPERIENCES OF THE JEWISH HOLIDAYS

Because there are several types of Judaism, there are many different ways to observe the Jewish holidays. Every Jew, therefore, has a different experience and memory regarding Jewish celebrations. U.S. Senator Joseph Lieberman comments that the Sabbath is of particular importance in his spiritual life. Lieberman and his wife, Hadassah, always observe the Sabbath (except in the case of emergencies) in order to focus on appreciating all that God has given them and to connect with their spiritual selves. In order to focus on the Sabbath, Lieberman does not even wear a watch on that day, does not answer the telephone, and does not watch television or listen to the radio. For many Jews, the weekly Sabbath is the most important Jewish holiday, since it occurs every week. It is a time when family members enjoy one another's company and are reminded of their religious traditions. The Sabbath is the first holiday that young children come to recognize since it is observed each week both at home and in the synagogue.

Next to the Sabbath, Passover is perhaps the most famous Jewish holiday. Many Jews who are otherwise unobservant celebrate Passover. For such Jews, like Rachael Byer of Seattle, Passover is a chance to engage in a ceremonial meal focused

WHY DO SOME JEWS EAT HAMAN'S EARS?

The holiday of Purim is one of the most festive and joyous celebrations of the Jewish year. It commemorates the time when the Jewish queen of the Persian Empire, Esther, intervened to save her people from annihilation. Haman, the prime minister of King Ahasuerus of Persia, was trying to exterminate the Jewish people. He cast lots, called "purim," to determine the day they would be destroyed. Because of Esther's intervention, Haman was hanged, and the Jewish people survived. Esther turned a day of doom into a day of gladness that was to be commemorated by a joyous celebration (Esther 9:22). Over time, various foods were created to celebrate Purim. One, called *hamantaschen*, is a pastry with three corners. It is filled with fruit, cheese, or poppy seeds. According to one tradition, it has three corners to remind Jews of the type of hat worn by Haman. Others claim that the three corners represent the three patriarchs: Abraham, Isaac, and Jacob. Hamantaschen is also called *"oznay Haman"* in Hebrew, which means "Haman's ears." In the past, it was a custom in Europe to cut off the ears of criminals before hanging them. Because Haman was hanged as a criminal, this pastry, which looks something like an ear, became known as Haman's ears.

See further, Alfred J. Kolatch, *The Jewish Book of Why*. Middle Village: Jonathan David, 1981, pp. 269–279.

on stories of hope and renewal. Passover, like the Sabbath, is a time of togetherness when the family sits down to a meal. Food is a very important aspect of Judaism. Jews look forward to the weekly Sabbath meal and the yearly Passover, where the foods symbolize important events in Jewish history. Michael Brown, reflecting on his experience growing up Jewish in Long Island, comments that, for him, Judaism had more to do with food than anything else!

Many contemporary Jews, like Michael Brown, have fond memories regarding food and especially Passover, which is the religious highlight of the year for many Jews. Passover features children in particular. Among the rituals that accompany the Passover meal are four questions, tradition- ally asked by the youngest child: Why does this night differ from all other nights? Why are only bitter herbs eaten on this night? Why are herbs dipped twice on this night? Why do we recline on this night and not on others? The adult in charge of the Passover Seder reads a response to these questions from the Haggadah, which explains the traditions and rituals behind the four questions.

Children also play an important role during the early part of the Seder, when a piece of matzo, called the *afikomon* (Greek for "dessert"), is placed in a napkin or bag. This matzo is passed out to the participants after the Passover meal and eaten as a dessert. Around seven hundred years ago, the custom arose of allowing children to steal the afikomon and hide it. Because the Seder could not continue until the afikomon was discovered, the leader of the Seder had to find it. He would customarily offer the children a gift in exchange for revealing the hiding place of the afikomon. This game was intended to make Passover more exciting and meaningful and to increase children's participation in this religious ritual.

In contemporary times, many Jews have begun to focus on story and the Jewish holidays as ways to live a righteous lifestyle. The concept of *tikkun olam*, Hebrew for "the repair of the world," has taken on particular importance. This concept goes back to the ancient rabbis, who taught that God's creation is sacred and should be respected. In recent times, the obscure holiday of *Tu B'Shevat*, originally a festival to separate one year from the next, has become a time to focus on the environment. In Israel, it is also known as Arbor (Tree) Day, and young school-children plant trees as part of the celebration. For Jews such as Matt Bier-Ariel, who has learned to connect this holiday with the concept of tikkun olam, taking care of the environment is a way to fulfill the Jewish calling of becoming a "light to the nations."

9

Memories

But Elsie found the strength to lift her arms to God and then felt a surge through her body; she knew then that they could do anything to her body to break it, but they could never invade her mind because she had her Lord.

—From the story of a Holocaust survivor
Source: "The Story of Elsie V.,"
remember.org. Available online at
http://www.remember.org/witness/elsiev.html.

Following the destruction of the Jerusalem Temple in A.D. 70, Jews increasingly settled in other regions throughout the Roman Empire. Over time, most Jews no longer lived in Israel. Jews who lived in the lands outside of Israel, referred to as the Diaspora, became the leaders of Jewish culture until the modern era. Jews in the Diaspora were frequently subjected to persecution. The problem that Jews have continually faced is how to live as a minority community in countries that are controlled by other religions.

Throughout history, Jews have encountered anti-Semitism. In order to survive, they have adopted a number of different strategies. They have attempted to live with their neighbors in peace, although this has been difficult at times. In order to assimilate and become more like their neighbors, some Jews adopted more liberal forms of religious practice. This has been the subject of much controversy within Judaism. Debates within the Jewish community led to the development of the different subdivisions of Judaism.

Because Jews were persecuted for centuries, the Jewish memory has largely been defined by suffering. In the twentieth century, the persecution of the Jews led to the creation of the first Jewish nation since the Roman period. The modern state of Israel was established by Jews who wanted to escape anti-Semitism in Europe. Memories of persecution continue to shape the religion, and the politics, of Israel to the present day. In order to understand contemporary Judaism, it is essential to understand some of the defining moments in history that continue to shape Jewish beliefs and practices today.

JUDAISM IN THE RABBINICAL ERA

The period between A.D. 70 and 1789 is known as the Rabbinical Era. During this time, the Jewish community wrote the Mishnah and the Talmud. The period ended when European Jews were granted equal rights with Gentiles. During this span of time, the Jewish people did not have a nation or a king of their own. Following the destruction of the Temple by the Romans in A.D. 70, the Diaspora widened, eliminating the center of Jewish intellectual activity. Religious leaders known as the *Genoim* established schools of Jewish learning. The city of Babylon, in modern Iraq, became one of the hubs of Jewish culture. Under the leadership of the Babylonian Genoim, the Babylonian Talmud emerged by the middle of the sixth century A.D.

Judaism has always shown a remarkable ability to adapt to new circumstances. When the Temple was first destroyed by the Babylonians in the sixth century B.C., Judaism began to focus on the study of scripture instead of sacrifice. When the rebuilt Temple was again destroyed in A.D. 70, this time by the Romans, Judaism once again became a religion of the book. The Tanakh, Mishnah, and Talmud became the major texts of Jewish religion and culture.

During the Middle Ages, Kabbalah Judaism emerged, based on a mystical interpretation of the Bible and the Talmud. This type of Judaism looks beyond the obvious meanings of a text. It teaches that religious books have hidden meanings that are known only to a select few. Jewish mysticism emphasizes angels, demons, magical spells, and charms—concepts that most Jews have traditionally ignored.

In Poland, another mystical form of Judaism emerged during the Rabbinical Era that rejected many teachings of Rabbinical Judaism. This movement was known as *Hasidism*, meaning "devotion" or "piety." Its followers were referred to as *Hasidim*, or "Pious Ones." The movement was founded by a rabbi named Israel Ben Eliezer (c. 1699–1760). He taught that God is not found primarily through scholarship and study, but through simple piety. His followers later began to call him the *Baal Shem Tov*, which means "Master of the Good Name," as a title of respect.

Compared to Rabbinical Judaism, Hasidism deemphasized the study of the Bible and Talmud. Instead, it stresses loving devotion to God, and obedience to a spiritual master called a *rebbe* (or *reb*). A spiritual master in Hasidic Judaism is also called a *tzaddik,* and is believed to have a special connection with God. According to this philosophy, the best way to practice Judaism is to follow the teachings and examples of a tzaddik. In Hasidic Judaism, each community is led by its own tzaddik, who is the spiritual and cultural leader of his community.

Hasidic Jews wear the traditional clothing of their ancestors in order to follow the ancient Jewish laws regarding food and purity. Because of their emphasis on purification, Hasidic Jewish communities generally live apart from Gentiles. In recent times, however, some Hasidic communities have become more open and live near, or work with, Gentiles.

Both Kabbalah and Hasidic Judaism emerged in areas where Jews faced much persecution by their Christian neighbors. The memory of the suffering and anti-Semitism that occurred during the Middle Ages continues to influence Jewish religion, culture, and politics today. Throughout the Middle Ages, the Christian Church was very powerful. Christian clergy of the time frequently taught that the Jews—and not the Roman officials who actually killed Jesus—were responsible for Jesus's death. This led to much anti-Semitism and persecution, and to violent attacks and murders known as pogroms. Jews were gradually restricted in their occupations and forced to live in areas of cities known as ghettos, surrounded by walls, in order to keep them apart from Christians. Jews were also banned from holding public office or marrying Christians. In A.D. 1215, the Church required Jews to wear special clothes and badges to show that they were not Christians. In many regions, Christians persecuted the Jews, and tried to forcibly convert them.

The Jewish community generally fared better under Islamic rule in the Middle East. Muslims regarded both Jews and Christians as "People of the Book," who were entitled to practice their own religions, because all three faiths share the same original scriptures. Islam is, to some extent, closer to Judaism and, therefore, welcomed it more than Christianity. Muslims do not believe that Jesus was the son of God or a divine being. Rather, Islam teaches that Jesus was a prophet. Islam rejects the Christian concept of the Trinity, which is the belief that God consists of three parts: the Father, Son, and Holy Spirit. Islam does not believe the Christian Trinity is monotheistic. Muslims view the concept of the Trinity as close to polytheism. Judaism, though, is strictly monotheistic and, like Islam, does not believe in the Trinity. The rejection of the Trinity was one religious belief that helped Jews live at peace in countries under Islamic rule.

In most Muslim countries, Jews lived in peace and prospered. Muslim Spain, for example, was a major center of Jewish culture, science, and thought. On some occasions, Muslims threatened their Jewish subjects and at times forced them to leave. Maimonides (A.D. 1135–1204), perhaps the greatest teacher in Jewish history, was forced to leave his home in Spain and move to Egypt. He became a prominent physician who treated the Muslim ruler of Egypt, and he wrote many influential religious books that are still read today. Despite occasional exceptions, however, Jews fared much better under Islam than under Christianity.

That situation has changed dramatically in recent years. Since the creation of the nation of Israel in 1948, Jews have frequently been persecuted in Muslim countries. Jews today experience severe conflict with their Muslim neighbors. Despite efforts to bring about peace, disputes over the rights to the land that makes of Israel continue to strain relations between contemporary Jews and Muslims.

REASONS FOR ANTI-SEMITISM

Christianity actually began as a form of Judaism. The Jews who followed Jesus believed that he was God's son and was resurrected from the dead after his crucifixion at the hands of the Romans. The first Christian community was still Jewish; it took about six decades for Christianity to completely separate from Judaism. The division between Judaism and Christianity largely took place when the Pharisees consolidated their hegemony over

Judaism, and Christians, who refused to follow the Pharisaic line, were defined as heretics by the Yavneh School.

Judaism is unique because its original Scriptures were adopted by both the Christian and Muslim religions. Each of these faiths teaches that it is the best guide to a correct understanding of the Jewish Scriptures. Both Christianity and Judaism teach that they possess the correct interpretation of the Jewish Scriptures. Christians wrote their own Scriptures, called the New Testament. They appended these writings to the Jewish Tanakh, which they renamed the Old Testament. The Christian writers of the New Testament frequently incorporated into the life of Jesus later debates and conflicts that they were having with the Jewish community over the correct interpretation of the Old Testament. Consequently, the Christian accounts of Jesus's life in the New Testament contain both stories about Jesus and interpretations of his teachings that reflect later debates between the followers of Jesus and other Jews.

The unfortunate consequence of the Christian adoption of the Tanakh has been centuries of Christian persecution of the Jews. This is in part because many Christians had trouble accepting a religion that disagreed with their own understanding of scripture. By the time the New Testament was written, the Christians were no longer recognized as Jews. The writers of the New Testament, despite the fact that many of them were former Jews, blamed the Jews for Jesus's death, not the Romans who actually sentenced Jesus to death and killed him, because Christianity was being persecuted by Rome. Christians, because they worshiped a man executed by the Romans for the crime of sedition, were considered dangerous. Judaism was a ancient and respected religious in the Roman Empire. New faiths, such as Christianity, were viewed as dangerous cults. The result of tensions between Jews and early Christians has been nearly twenty centuries of Christian-backed anti-Semitism. In recent decades, however, nearly all major branches of both Catholic and Protestant Christianity have renounced anti-Semitism and apologized for the past crimes and unjust teachings of Christianity.

JUDAISM'S CHANGING SITUATION

Jews who lived in Christian countries were persecuted for many centuries. Christian rulers, however, usually allowed Jewish communities some degree of autonomy. Even with limited freedom, in some areas, the Jewish community prospered.

In general, however, life in Europe was difficult because the Christian Church continued to teach that the Jewish people were responsible for the death of Jesus. By the end of the fifteenth century, the Jewish people had been either persecuted or officially expelled in nearly every country in Europe. Jews were expelled from England in 1290, from Germany in the fourteenth century, from France in 1306, and from Spain in 1492. Many Jewish refugees fled to Eastern European countries, such as Poland, where they were permitted to enter some vocations that had been closed to them in other countries. By the end of the sixteenth century, Poland had the world's largest Jewish population, with more than half a million.

In the sixteenth century, Europe changed dramatically with the Protestant Reformation. This movement, which had its origins in the teachings of Martin Luther, led to a split in Christianity between Catholics and newly formed Protestant sects. Luther's followers rejected the authority of the pope, the leader of the Catholic Church, as well as many traditional Christian practices and teachings. His supporters also abandoned any teachings or practices that they could not find in the text of the New Testament. At first, Luther denounced the Catholic Church for its persecution of the Jews. Unfortunately, Luther later adopted anti-Semitism himself and wrote a book that urged the persecution of Jews.

The Catholic Church, after the establishment of Protestant Christianity, underwent a period of change known as the Counter-Reformation. The Church, nevertheless, did not abandon many of its anti-Jewish teachings. Jews in Rome were still forced to live in a ghetto. Both Catholic and Protestant Christians continued to persecute local Jewish communities for centuries after Luther's death in 1546.

During the eighteenth century, Europe went through a series of political and social changes known as the Enlightenment. This broad philosophical movement resulted in better conditions for Jews. Influenced by advances in science and emerging European nationalism, the thinkers of the Enlightenment placed less emphasis on past tradition, and advocated tolerance. The French Revolution, which began in 1789, is perhaps the best-known example. In 1791, the French National Assembly granted Jews full rights as citizens. Jews were then free to worship as they pleased. This emancipation spread to other countries in Europe, where some restrictions against Jews were gradually removed. In many regions, the ghettos were torn down, and Jews began to occupy important political and social positions.

Judaism during the Enlightenment was undergoing a revolution of its own. Some Jews were swept up by the scientific spirit of the age and wanted to modernize Judaism. Unlike Kabbalah and Hasidic Judaism, both of which tended to promote separation from Gentiles, this new interpretation of Judaism taught that Jews must adapt in order to live among non-Jews. Several thinkers argued that the mission of the Jews was to remind all people of the ethical duties required by God. A German Jew named Moses Mendelssohn (1729–1786) started a movement known as the Jewish Enlightenment, which attempted to integrate Jews more fully into European culture. Mendelssohn thought that Jews should no longer live as their ancestors had done, but should become full members of European society. He believed that Jews should speak the national language of the places in which they lived and dress and act like other citizens. These changes led to the creation of Reform Judaism, which caused other Jews to reexamine their own religious beliefs.

ZIONISM

Thanks to the advances generated during the Enlightenment, Jews in Europe thought they were finally full and equal citizens. Unfortunately, anti-Semitism still existed. The word *anti-*

Semitism was first coined around 1870 by German writer Wilhelm Marr (1818–1904). He taught that the Jewish people were of a different race that was inferior to pure-blooded Germans. The term has since been used generally to describe all kinds of anti-Jewish thoughts and actions. In order to spread anti-Semitism, some people wrote fictitious books. The most famous is a work known as *The Protocols of the Elders of Zion,* which claimed to document a secret Jewish organization that was attempting to take control of the world. This book circulated throughout Russia and other nations during the late 1880s. During this period, Jews gradually began to face increased persecution and pogroms throughout Europe.

In 1894, a trial took place in France that changed Judaism forever. A French army captain named Alfred Dreyfus was accused of betraying his country by giving away military secrets during the Franco-Prussian War of 1870–1871. It became apparent to many people during the trial that Dreyfus was innocent, and was being persecuted simply because he was Jewish. Still, Dreyfus was convicted, given a life sentence, and sent to the infamous French prison on Devil's Island. After much public outcry by several prominent French intellectuals, he was later released. An Austrian Jewish journalist named Theodor Herzl covered the Dreyfus trial for his newspaper. Herzl realized that anti-Semitism in Europe had not disappeared. He looked to history, and came to the belief that the Jewish people would never be free from persecution unless they had their own country. The idea of establishing a Jewish homeland became known as Zionism.

With the memories of centuries of persecution in their minds, increasing numbers of Jews were drawn to Herzl's teachings. Many thought there was no future or safety for Jews in Europe. Taking matters into their own hands, they organized the First Zionist Conference in Basel, Switzerland, in 1897. At first, there were debates over where Jews should settle. Because of Israel's importance in the Tanakh, most Jews believed that the region then known as Palestine should become the Jewish homeland. In the early 1900s, Jews slowly began to purchase land and develop settlements in Palestine. To escape persecution, they began to gradually move from Europe to Palestine.

Life was not easy in Palestine. Following World War I (1914–1918), the British took control of the region, which had previously been part of the Turkish Ottoman Empire. The Muslim community put pressure on the European powers to restrict Jewish immigration, so as not to allow further increase in the number of Jews in Palestine. The British government responded by setting limits on how many Jews would be allowed to move to Palestine. This left many European Jews with no place to go, to escape persecution, since countries such as the United States banned large numbers of Jews from immigrating. With Europe closed, and shipping routes either closed or too dangerous for commercial travel, Palestine was considered the only safe country for Jews.

THE HOLOCAUST

The Holocaust is without doubt the most important event in modern Jewish history. The memory of the Holocaust is firmly etched in the consciousness of all Jews, and it continues to define Jewish religion, culture, and politics to the present day. The word *Holocaust* ("burnt sacrificial offering") comes from the Latin word *holocaustum*, the Greek word *holocaust*, and the Hebrew word *Shoah* ("annihilation"). The term refers to the murder of approximately 6 million Jews by the leaders of Germany, from 1939 until Germany's surrender in World War II in 1945.

The Holocaust was not something entirely new. Rather, it was the culmination of centuries of anti-Semitism. It was made more tragic, though, because it took place in modern Europe. In 1933, Adolf Hitler became the chancellor of Germany and adopted a political platform based on anti-Semitism. Over time, Hitler's Nazi Party began to persecute Jews. In 1935, the Nuremberg laws made Jews second-class citizens, thereby undoing in one act nearly all the advances Jews had made during the preceding centuries. Jews in Germany were required to wear special insignia to show that they were Jewish. Jewish businesses were forcibly taken over by non-Jews. Anti-Semitism spread to Austria and Poland after the Nazis took control of these countries. On November 9–10, 1938, known as *Kristallnacht* ("the Night of Broken Glass"), synagogues and Jewish businesses throughout Germany were destroyed.

In 1942, the situation in Germany changed when the Nazis' so-called "Final Solution" went into effect. Hitler's government set out to kill Europe's entire Jewish population. Jews were forcibly transported to concentration camps, where they were starved, tortured, asphyxiated by poison gas, or worked to death as slave laborers. Approximately one-third of the world's Jewish population was exterminated during the Holocaust. After World War II, in 1946, many of those who had been responsible for the Holocaust were tried and executed in the German city of Nuremberg. Although the trials attempted to bring some of the Nazi leaders to justice, it was too late to undo the damage their work had done. The Jewish population would never fully recover its incalculable losses. In fact, many regions in Europe today no longer have any Jewish residents because of the Holocaust.

The Holocaust brought about a renewed interest in Zionism. Many Jews no longer believed that they could live in Europe

THE CHOSEN PEOPLE

We have not chosen God; he has chosen us. There is no concept of a chosen God but there is the idea of a chosen people. The idea of a chosen people does not suggest the preference for a people based upon discrimination among a number of peoples. We do not say that we are a superior people. The "chosen people" means a people approached and chosen by God. The significance of this term is genuine in relation to God rather than in relation to other peoples. It signifies not a quality inherent in the people but a relationship between the people and God.

From Abraham Joshua Heschel, *God in Search of Man: A Philosophy of Judaism.* New York: Farrar, Straus and Giroux, 1955, pp. 425–426.

without persecution. With no homes to return to, and fearful of renewed persecution, many European Jews moved to Palestine in a sudden influx of Jews escaping from Europe after the end of World War II. As the Jews' numbers increased, tensions between the Jews and Muslims in Palestine increased, too. The result was a war with the Arab-Muslim population in Palestine and the surrounding countries that created a state of hostility that still exists today. The United Nations (UN) tried to resolve the situation by dividing Palestine into Jewish and Arab regions in 1948. Although the Jews accepted the plan, the Muslims did not. On May 14, 1948, the new, independent nation of Israel was declared. The very next day, Israel's Arab neighbors united to wage war against the new Jewish state. By the end of May, after Israel's great military success in its war for independence, a truce was called. The Jewish homeland was officially its own nation.

Countries such as the United States and the Soviet Union recognized Israel as a country right after its creation in 1948. Today, Israel is the world's only Jewish nation. Many Jews around the world see it as a safe homeland for Jews who wish to escape persecution.

In both Israel and in other places around the world, the Holocaust is commemorated each year on Holocaust Remembrance Day, celebrated on the twenty-seventh day of Nissan, the first month of the Jewish calendar. Because some of those who survived the Holocaust are still alive, the events of that tragic time remain a living part of Jewish memory today. This legacy continues to shape politics in Israel, as the country's leaders frequently act in ways that they believe will keep Jewish citizens of the country safe from danger and persecution.

10

Judaism in the World Today

*We are living in a time when there is an
unprecedented opportunity to make our region
a good place for our people to live in.
It is the Genesis. Try we must. Try we do.*

—Former Israeli Prime Minister
Shimon Peres, January 10, 1996

ontemporary Judaism continues to be shaped by developments in the modern state of Israel. The ongoing tension between Israelis and Palestinians has forced many Jews to reexamine their religious beliefs. In recent decades, many Jews who live in Israel have debated the issue of who is a Jew. Jews in the United States and elsewhere around the world continue to discuss the future of Judaism, and the relationship between the Jewish community in the Diaspora and Jews in Israel. Though Orthodox Judaism still follows the traditional definition that a Jew is a person with a Jewish mother, an increasing number of Jews are nonobservant. Many are not even recognized as Jewish by Orthodox rabbis, despite the fact that they consider themselves Jewish. Orthodox Judaism at first rejected the existence of the state of Israel, since the Orthodox believed that only God could bring it about. Because humans created it, they did not consider it a valid country. In recent decades, however, many Orthodox Jews have become active in Israeli politics. Some have sought to pass legislation that would require the government to recognize as Jews only people who fit the Orthodox definition of Judaism. Different branches of Judaism, moreover, continue to debate the issue of conversion, and what a person must do to become Jewish.

Because there are so many definitions of Judaism, there are many answers to questions about Israel, Jewish identity, and conversion. Judaism has shown that it is a very versatile faith by surviving many persecutions and forced displacements of its population. Even at the present time, Judaism is undergoing changes as it continues to adapt to the modern world. The problem of assimilation is a current topic of debate in the Jewish community, since more Jews are no longer observant and are, therefore, often indistinguishable from Gentiles. Because there are many different ways to practice Judaism, there will always be disagreement within the Jewish community about what it means to be Jewish. Judaism in the future will undoubtedly change and adapt to meet new problems, just as it has always changed since its very beginning. Despite

Judaism's diversity, all Jews in the world today must deal with certain topics currently under debate by the worldwide Jewish community, such as the Messiah and the nation of Israel. These issues continue to both unite and divide the subdivisions of Judaism today.

PAST PROMISES AND ISRAEL

Judaism has traditionally taught that God would one day send a Messiah to usher in a new world that would be free of evil. The famed Jewish teacher Maimonides even considered the belief in the Messiah a central principle of Judaism. Many rabbis taught that the Messiah would bring a golden age of happiness, restore justice, and teach the Torah. At that time, the Jewish people would return to the land of Israel, and Jerusalem would again become the spiritual center of Judaism.

More progressive Jews rejected the traditional belief in the Messiah and the literal return to Zion. They preferred to speak of a "Messianic Age" in which peace and righteousness would be established. This golden age is something that humans must bring about through their own efforts. Because Judaism existed for nearly two thousand years without its own country, many Jews no longer believe that Israel is essential for the survival of Judaism, or that a Messiah will come to relieve Jewish suffering. For these Jews, the establishment of the modern state of Israel was an important political event, but it does not necessarily portend the coming of the Messiah and the end of the age. Israel is important to Jews around the world spiritually because it is considered the only country in which Jews are safe from persecution. For this reason, most Jews believe Israel must be supported, even though they do not think a Jewish nation is necessary for the survival of Judaism. Other Jews, whether religious or secular, who live in Israel believe it is vital to the survival of Judaism since, if it disappears, it could mean the beginning of another cycle of persecution like the Holocaust.

THE PROBLEM OF EVIL

Judaism in modern times has reassessed many of its most cherished beliefs. In addition to such concepts as the Messiah, Judaism has been forced to address the problems of evil and suffering. During the period of the Tanakh, Jews did not believe in an afterlife. The concepts of heaven, hell, and resurrection largely developed during and following the Exile. Resurrection is only clearly articulated in the biblical Book of Daniel. After the biblical period, Jews developed a belief in the afterlife and resurrection. During the Middle Ages, the belief that the dead would be resurrected in the Messianic Age and judged for their deeds became a central tenet of Judaism. Many Orthodox Jews still maintain this belief, and expect the righteous to enter heaven and the wicked to go to a place of eternal punishment. This hope helped Judaism survive many centuries of persecution, because it maintained that, despite present suffering, there would be justice in the next life. Today, many liberal Jews have rejected the idea of divine punishment in an afterlife. Reform and Conservative Judaism accept the belief in an immortal soul, but neither precisely defines what this means. Some liberal Jews have even rejected the idea that God will intervene in the world to remedy current problems. For these more liberal, or secular, Jews, Judaism is a faith that is dedicated to improving conditions on Earth.

Judaism and the other Western religions continue to struggle to explain the problem of evil. Judaism traditionally teaches that God will triumph over evil, and it emphasizes that Jews are largely a people united with God by a covenant. Judaism has never taught that religion guarantees happiness.

During the Exile, Judaism developed a new explanation of evil. Because God is good, God cannot be responsible for evil. Instead, Judaism used the concept of Satan to account for the presence of evil in the world. For many Jews, evil is the absence of good. Judaism stresses that humans are responsible for their own conduct. Judaism teaches that God gives humans complete freedom to be good or evil—freedom of choice. This means that God is not responsible for evil. It is humans who are to blame.

The Holocaust forced many Jews to reassess traditional explanations of evil. Because the Holocaust was such a horrible event, some Jews have maintained that it either proves that God does not exist, or that God does not care about humanity. If either of these is the case, they assert, then the Jewish people must look to their community of faith for meaning. According to this interpretation, Judaism is a cultural heritage. Jews can still follow the values of Judaism, but are not required to adhere to the traditional laws of the Bible and the Talmud.

Another post-Holocaust explanation holds that God is in the world and suffers along with humanity. According to this perspective, God is not omnipotent. Instead, God is limited like humans and is capable of suffering, too.

Jews continue to debate the meaning of the Holocaust and the nature of God. Christians have also been forced to examine their role in the Holocaust, because many churches did little to stop it. In the years after the Holocaust, all major

WHY?

To try to explain the Holocaust, or any suffering, as God's will is to side with the executioner rather than with his victim, and to claim that God does the same. I cannot make sense of the Holocaust by taking it to be God's will. Even if I could accept the death of an innocent individual now and then without having to rethink all of my beliefs, the Holocaust represents too many deaths, too much evidence against the view that "God is in charge and He has His reasons." I have to believe that the Holocaust was at least as much of an offense to God's moral order as it is to mine, or how can I respect God as a source of moral guidance?

From Harold S. Kushner, *When Bad Things Happen to Good People*. New York: Avon Books, 1981, p. 82.

branches of Christianity began a dialogue with the Jewish community in hopes of preventing future violence and as a way to learn more about the common traditions shared by Judaism and Christianity.

ISRAEL AND PALESTINE

The creation of the Jewish state of Israel is the most important historical event that has taken place since the Holocaust. Israel was, in part, shaped and created because of the Holocaust. The Jews who helped establish the modern nation of Israel believed that the Jewish people needed a homeland of their own in order to survive. Israel continues to be a haven for Jews who face persecution in their own countries. It also attracts many Jews from around the world who seek, for various reasons, to live in the ancestral Jewish homeland.

In the early days of settlement, some Jews created a new type of village known as a *kibbutz*. The first kibbutz was established in Deganyah, adjacent to the Sea of Galilee, in 1910. A kibbutz is a collective agricultural settlement based on socialist principles. There is no private property on a kibbutz. Everything is owned in common, and all members perform physical labor in the fields or factories. Although few people in modern Israel live on a kibbutz, those who do remain very active in political and social causes. Today, many foreigners volunteer to live for a time on a kibbutz in order to experience this unusual lifestyle.

The establishment of Israel continues to create problems for the worldwide Jewish community. Many Palestinians were displaced in 1948 when Israel fought the surrounding Arab nations for its survival. Since then, Israel has been in a state of conflict with many of its Arab neighbors. Wars have frequently erupted, resulting in increased anti-Semitic feelings in the Middle East. In 1967, Israel fought the Six-Day War against several of its Arab neighbors, and unexpectedly captured land from Jordan, Egypt, and Syria. During this war, Israel also took possession of the city of Jerusalem.

Israel now considers Jerusalem its capital city, although many countries dispute this claim. Israel continues to occupy the territories it captured in 1967, areas known as the West Bank, the Gaza Strip, and the Golan Heights. The return of these lands to the Palestinians and other countries remains an issue that divides the Jewish community in Israel and around the world today.

Jews also debate the problem of tension between the Jews in Israel and the Palestinians, who want to establish their own nation of Palestine. Most Palestinians are Muslims, although there is still a small Palestinian Christian community in Israel. Some Jews are strong supporters of Israel, and believe that the nation is the future of Judaism. Initially after the creation of Israel, Jewish support for the new nation was strong, largely because of the tragic events of the Holocaust. Many countries, such as the United States and the former Soviet Union, recognized Israel as the Jewish homeland. Over time, though, Jewish support for Israel has been divided. Some Jews do not believe that Israel is essential for the survival of their faith. In recent decades, many have argued that Israel should return the occupied territories and help the Palestinian people create their own country. Efforts at peace have not been successful. In November 1995, Israeli Prime Minister Yitzhak Rabin (1922–1995) was assassinated for his efforts to make peace with the Palestinians. Because the United States has a large Jewish population (and a Muslim population of roughly the same size), Israel continues to occupy an important place in American foreign policy. In recent times, more Arab nations have shown a willingness to accept peace with Israel, in order to resolve the Palestinian problem.

Judaism in Israel is in a state of flux. Whereas Jews in the United States are predominantly liberal, in Israel, Judaism is very diverse. The country continues to change as a result of immigration, most recently from the former Soviet Union. Many of the newcomers are from more secular

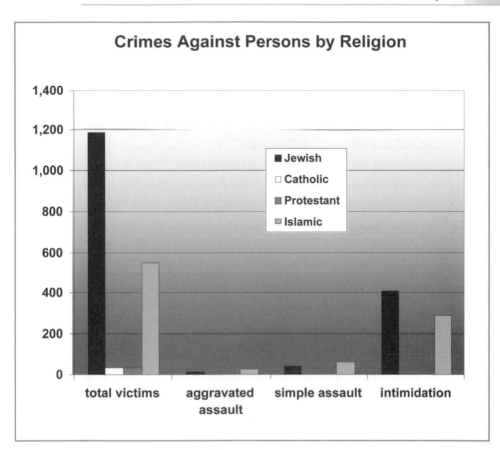

Crimes Against Persons by Religion

Legend:
- Jewish
- Catholic
- Protestant
- Islamic

X-axis categories: total victims, aggravated assault, simple assault, intimidation

Y-axis: 0, 200, 400, 600, 800, 1,000, 1,200, 1,400

Despite the fact that the Jewish religion advocates nonviolence and tolerance of other religions, because they are a minority, Jews have often been targeted by those who commit hate crimes. Even in the United States, where religious freedom has always been a fundamental right, Jews continue to face threats from people who attack them solely because of their religion. According to this information adapted from the FBI's Uniform Crime Reporting Program in 2001, other religious groups have been the targets of hate crimes, but Jewish people have by far suffered the most incidents.

backgrounds, although they have suffered decades of anti-Semitism. Orthodox rabbis in Israel (who are not very powerful politically) do not recognize many of these immigrants as Jewish.

Israel at first attracted many secular Jews, but now is attracting a disproportionate number of religious extremists. This is especially true in Jerusalem, where about one-third of the population is said to be of this persuasion. This trend worries more moderate Jews, including the Israeli government.

THE CHANGING FACE OF JUDAISM

Judaism in the United States continues to influence Jews throughout the world. Although the Jewish population of the United States was just over 2 percent in 2001, Jews continue to exert a major role in American society through their political and cultural contributions. The Holocaust Museum in Washington, D.C., serves not only as a reminder of the events of the Holocaust, but is also an institution dedicated to combating all forms of injustice, racism, and religious persecution. Jews continue to play central roles in politics and in championing social causes.

Perhaps the greatest change in recent times is the increased assimilation of the Jewish community. More Jews than ever are now either secular, or have largely abandoned Judaism as a result of marriage to non-Jews. There are several reasons for the decline of Jewish practice. In the past, when Jews were still subject to discrimination, some families in the United States hid their Jewishness and became secular. Others have adopted more liberal interpretations of Judaism, and regard it as a tradition rather than a religion. They may observe some Jewish holidays, but do not attend synagogue on a regular basis. Because their numbers are difficult to determine, it is impossible to give a firm estimate of the Jewish population in the United States.

Some Jews have expressed alarm at the growing assimilation of the Jewish community, while others believe that the face of Judaism should change to be more accepting of converts and people who are secular. Jews continue to debate the influence, if any, that Israel should have on Jews in the United States.

Because Judaism has survived through many periods when it looked as though it might disappear from history, most Jews believe that their religion will always exist. Judaism's tendency to adapt to circumstances and the strength of its convictions have enabled it to survive centuries of persecution. Judaism is a religion that will undoubtedly continue to change and make significant contributions to world history.

Judaism is the foundation of the great monotheistic faiths—Judaism, Christianity, and Islam—which together account for more than half of the world's population. Its ethical code is a source for both religious and secular law, especially in the West but to some extent around the globe. Judaism may not be one of the world's largest religions, but its influence greatly exceeds its numbers.

1900–1700 B.C.	The Age of the Patriarchs: Abraham, Isaac, Jacob
1800–1900 B.C.	Abraham's departure from Ur to Canaan
c. 1250 B.C.	Exodus from Egypt
1000–900 B.C.	The United Kingdom: David and Solomon
900–850 B.C.	The Divided Kingdom: Nations of Israel and Judah
721 B.C.	Northern kingdom of Israel destroyed by the Assyrians
586–539 B.C.	Destruction of Jerusalem Temple by Babylonians, and Exile

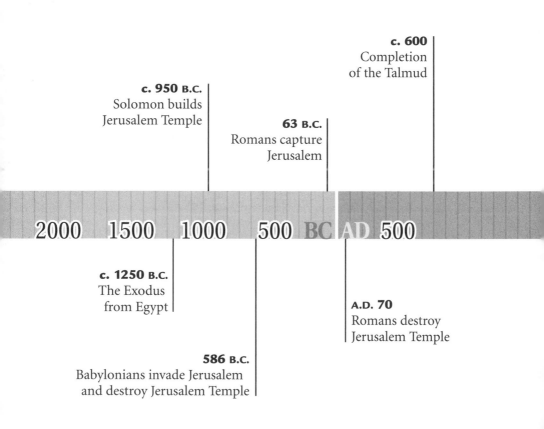

c. 600
Completion
of the Talmud

c. 950 B.C.
Solomon builds
Jerusalem Temple

63 B.C.
Romans capture
Jerusalem

2000   1500   1000   500 BC AD 500

c. 1250 B.C.
The Exodus
from Egypt

A.D. 70
Romans destroy
Jerusalem Temple

586 B.C.
Babylonians invade Jerusalem
and destroy Jerusalem Temple

538–400 B.C. Return from Exile, and Restoration: Return to Jerusalem and rebuilding of the Temple

400–100 B.C. Hellenistic Era: Period of the Maccabean Wars and Jewish Kingdom

63 B.C.–A.D. 565 Roman Era: The Rabbinical Era

A.D. 630–1095 Islamic rule in Israel

1095–1199 Crusades period

1200–1917 Return of Israel to Islamic rule

1791 Emancipation of all Jews of France

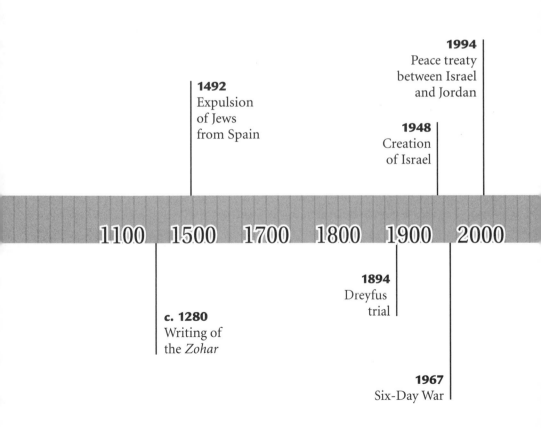

1994 Peace treaty between Israel and Jordan

1492 Expulsion of Jews from Spain

1948 Creation of Israel

1100 1500 1700 1800 1900 2000

c. 1280 Writing of the *Zohar*

1894 Dreyfus trial

1967 Six-Day War

CHRONOLOGY

1886 Herzl publishes his book proposing a Jewish state

1917–1948 British control of Israel/Palestine

1939–1945 Holocaust

1948 Creation of the state of Israel

1967 Six-Day War

1994 Peace treaty between Israel and Jordan

1995 Assassination of Israeli Prime Minister Yitzhak Rabin

2003 President George W. Bush makes efforts to resolve Israeli and Palestinian conflict

BOOKS

Cohn-Sherbok, Dan. *Judaism.* Prentice Hall, 1999.

Fisher, Mary Pat. *Living Religions*, 5th ed. Prentice-Hall, 2002.

Frank, Anne. *The Diary of a Young Girl.* Pocket Books, 1952.

Koester, Helmut. *Introduction to the New Testament.* vol. 1. Fortress Press, 1982.

Kolatch, Alfred J. *The Jewish Book of Why.* Jonathan David, 1981.

Molloy, Michael. *Experiencing the World's Religions: Tradition, Challenge, and Change*, 2nd ed. Mayfield, 2002.

Potok, Chaim. *The Chosen.* Fawcett Crest, 1967.

Seltzer, Robert M. *Jewish People, Jewish Thought: The Jewish Experience in History.* Macmillan, 1980.

Sharfman, Harold. *The Frontier Jews: An Account of Jewish Pioneers and Settlers in Early America.* The Citadel Press, 1978.

Trepp, Leo. *The Complete Book of Jewish Observance.* Behrman House/ Summit Books, 1980.

Unterman, Alan. *Jews: Their Religious Beliefs and Practices.* Routledge & Keegan Paul, 1981.

Wiesel, Elie. *Memoirs: All Rivers Run to the Sea.* Schocken, 1995.

———. *One Generation After.* Avon, 1965.

BIBLIOGRAPHY

WEBSITES

Biers-Ariel, Matt, "Jews and Nature."
http://www.jewishfamily.com/jc/holidays/tu_bshevat/jews_nature.txt.

Brown, Michael J. "Revlections of the Congregation: Growing Up Jewish on Long Island."
http://ww.bethelsudbury.org/reflect/guj.htm.

Carlson, Charles. "Lithuania/Ukraine: Karaims Struggle to Maintain Their Language and Culture."
http://www.rferl.org/nca/features/2003/07/22072003165742.asp.

Cohen, Edward. "The Peddler's Grandson: Growing Up Jewish in Mississippi."
http://www.peddlersgrandson.com/excerpt.html.

Grodsky, Phyllis B. "My Father's Quest."
http://www.jewishmag.com/69mag/fathersquest/fathersquest.htm.

Iwasaki, John. "Seder Gives Young Jews a Place to Connect." *Seattle Post-Intelligencer*, April 17, 2003.
http://seattlepi.nwsource.com/local/117958_passover17.html.

Jewish Virtual Library
http://www.us-israel.org/jsource/History/jewpop2.html.

Jews.Net
http://www.jews.net/index.htm.

"Kabbalah-Judaism's Way into the New Age."
http://www.tmtestimony.org.uk/library/2000_10.htm.

"Madonna Buys £3.5 Million London House for Kabbalah Centre."
Hello Magazine, July 30, 2003.
http://www.hellomagazine.com/2003/05/26/madonna.

Meyers, Nechemia. "Israel's 30,000 Karaites follow Bible, not Talmud."
http://www.jewishf.com/bk991210/lackariate.shtml.

PRIMARY SOURCES

Frank, Anne. *The Diary of a Young Girl*. Pocket Books, 1952.

Rodney, Rabbi Mariner, ed. *The Torah*. Henry Holt & Company, Inc., 1997.

Steinsaltz, Adin, ed. *The Essential Talmud*. Jason Aronson, 1992.

Strack, Herman L. *Introduction to the Talmud and Midrash*, trans. Markus Bockmuehl. Fortress Press, 1992.

Wiesel, Elie. *Memoirs: All Rivers Run to the Sea*. Schocken, 1995.

———. *One Generation After*. Avon, 1965.

SECONDARY SOURCES

Cohn-Sherbok, Dan. *Judaism*. Prentice Hall, 1999.

Kolatch, Alfred J. *The Jewish Book of Why*. Jonathan David, 1981.

Seltzer, Robert M. *Jewish People, Jewish Thought: The Jewish Experience in History*. Macmillan, 1980.

Sharfman, Harold. *The Frontier Jews: An Account of Jewish Pioneers and Settlers in Early America*. The Citadel Press, 1978.

Trepp, Leo. *Judaism: Development and Life*, 4th ed. Wadsworth, 2000.

WEBSITES

Jewish Virtual Library
http://www.us-israel.org/jsource/judaism.html
An online research center with resources about Jewish history and culture, as well as news and developments in United States–Israel activities.

Judaism 101
http://www.jewfaq.org/
An online resource with information on Jewish history, customs, beliefs, and scripture.

FURTHER READING

Orthodox Union

http://www.ou.org/

An online resource for information about the history, beliefs, and rules and regulations of Orthodox Judaism.

Reform Judaism

http://rj.org/

The official site of the Reform movement, outlining its history, beliefs, and conditions for membership.

The United Synagogue of Conservative Judaism

http://www.uscj.org/

An organization that seeks to unite all congregations that practice Conservative Judaism and to provide information about Conservative Judaism's roots and beliefs.

INDEX

INDEX

Germany
  and Ashkenazi Jews, 8-9
  Jews in, 11, 106
  and Reform Judaism, 15.
  See also Holocaust
ghettos, 6, 103, 106, 107
Ginsberg, Allen, 86
girls
  and Bat Mitzvah, 74, 80
  birth of, 72
  and education, 73.
  See also women
glass, in marriage ceremony, 75-76
God
  and covenant with Abraham, 3,
    6, 20-24, 27, 34-35, 40, 44, 53,
    55, 57, 71, 72, 115
  and David, 31-32, 35
  descriptions of, 49, 50
  and Exodus, 24-31, 56, 93
  and good and evil, 53-55, 115-
    117
  with Jewish people, 52-53, 72
  and Jewish Scriptures, 37
  Jewish view of, 49-52
  and Jews as chosen people, 52
  and judges, 31
  and Maimonides's principles,
    50-52
  and monotheism, 3, 19, 20-21,
    22, 28-29, 49, 53, 54-55, 68
  and Moses, 26-30
  nature of, 50-51
  and prophets, 32, 33, 56
  and relationship with humans,
    51-52
  and relationship with Jewish
    people, 50-51
  and Saul, 30
  and Torah, 51, 55-56, 92-93
godmother, 71-72
Golan Heights, 118
Goliath, 31
Gomorrah, 55

good and evil, and theodicy, 53-55
Goodman, Benny, 85
Great Britain, and Palestine, 108-
  109
Greece
  and Hanukkah, 95-96
  and Sephardic Jews, 8
greens, and Pesach, 93
Grodsky, Phyllis, 79-80
growing up Jewish, 70-81
  and adulthood, 74-76
  and Bar Mitzvah, 73-74
  and circumcision, 6, 22, 30, 53,
    71-72
  and death and burial, 76-77
  and education, 73
  and marriage, 74-76
  personal experiences of, 77-81
  and Pidyan Ha-Ben, 72-73

Habakkuk, 41
Haftarah, 67
Hagar, 22-23
Haggadah, 44, 98
Haggai, 41
hair, and Orthodox Judaism, 12, 73
halakhah, 44
Haman, 96, 97
Hanukkah, 64, 91, 95-96
Hasidic Judaism, 83, 102-103, 107
Hawn, Goldie, 87
head covering
  and Conservative Judaism, 13-14
  and Orthodox Judaism, 12-13
  and Reform Judaism, 14-15
Hebrew Bible, 37.
  See also Bible
Hebrew language, 7, 8, 12, 20, 65,
  68
Hebrew name, 72
Hebrews, 20
  and Abraham, 21
  and Conquest, 30-31
  and Exodus, 24-30, 40

INDEX

INDEX

Safed, and Kabbalah, 47
Sagan, Carl, 86
Salinger, J.D., 86
salt, and Pesach, 93
Samaritans, 9-10
sandek (godfather), 71
Sanders, Samuel, 84
Sarah, 22-23, 24
Satan (or devil), 54, 115
Saul, 31-32
Schindler's List (film), 86
scribes, 59-60, 63
scrolls, and Tanakh, 42.
    See also Torah scroll
Sea of Reeds, 28
secular Jews, 5-6, 16-17, 77, 115,
    118, 120
Seder, 93, 98
Seinfeld, Jerry, 87
Seinfeld (television show), 87
Semites, 20
Sephardic Judaism, 8, 9, 68, 84
sermon, 60
shadkan (marriage brokers), 75
Shavuot, 93-94
Shearith Israel, 84
Sheba, Queen of, 9
Shekhinah, 46, 49
Shema, 49, 68, 76
shiva, 77
Shoah, 109.
    See also Holocaust
shofar, 94
shul, 62
Sicily, Jews of, 69
Siddur, 65
siddurim, 63
side-curls, 12, 73
Simeon bar Yohai, 46
Simhat Torah ("Joy in Torah"),
    95
Sinai Desert, 38, 40, 95
Sinai, Mount, 26-27, 28-30, 35,
    40, 43-44, 93-94

Sinai Peninsula, 26
Six-Day War, 117
social justice, 56, 57, 59
Sodom, 55
Solomon, 9, 32, 35, 41
"Song of Songs," 41
Sophie's Choice (film), 86
soul, immortal, 115
Spain, Jews in, 6, 8, 104, 106
Spanish language, and Ladino, 8
Splendor, Book of. *See* Zohar
Star of David, 64
Steel, Danielle, 86
story, role of, 19
    and history, 18-35
    and Jewish tradition, 77-81, 83
Streisand, Barbara, 86
Stuyvesant, Peter, 84
sukkah, 95
Sukkoth (Feast of the Tabernacles),
    93, 95
synagogue, 58-69
    in American history, 84
    buildings for, 60
    and depictions of God, 49
    design for, 60-63
    and furnishings, 63-65, 83
    and history of Judaism, 59
    interior of, 61
    and meaning of term, 59
    and mikveh, 60
    offices and liturgy in, 68-69
    origins of, 59-60
    and secular Jews, 5-6
    and shoe removal by Karaites, 11
    worship in, 12, 61-63, 65-69, 92
Syrians, and Hanukkah, 91, 95-96

Tabernacle, 30, 64
Taheb (Messiah), and Samaritans,
    10
talit (prayer shawl), 66, 69, 73
Talmud, 11, 14, 15, 44-46, 47, 83,
    101, 102

138

INDEX

Page:

B: © Réunion des Musées Nationaux/Art Resource, NY

B: © Scala/Art Resource, NY

C: © Erich Lessing/ Art Resource, NY

D: © The Pierpont Morgan Library/Art Resource, NY

E: © Erich Lessing/ Art Resource, NY

E: © Erich Lessing/ Art Resource, NY

F: © Arte & Immagini srl/ CORBIS

G: © Archivo Iconografico, S. A./ CORBIS

H: Courtesy of the Library of Congress Geography and Map Division

5: Adapted from information found at the World Jewish Congress

119: Adapted from information in the 2001, FBI Uniform Crime Reporting Program

Cover: © The Jewish Museum, NY/Art Resource, NY

Frontis: Courtesy of the Library of Congress Geography and Map Division

DR. KENNETH ATKINSON holds an M.A. and a Ph.D. in biblical literature from Temple University, and a Master of Divinity degree from the University of Chicago. An assistant professor of religion at the University of Northern Iowa, he is the author of *An Intertextual Study of the Psalms of Solomon* (Edwin Mellen Press, 2001), *Introduction to World Religions* (College Network, 2002), and *I Cried to the Lord* (E.J. Brill, 2004). His scholarly writings on biblical literature and the Dead Sea Scrolls have appeared in *The Interpretation of Scripture in Early Judaism and Christianity, Journal of Biblical Literature, Journal for the Study of the Pseudepigrapha, New Testament Studies, Biblical Archaeological Review, Paradigms, Criterion, Review of Biblical Literature, Religious Studies Review,* and *Critical Review of Books in Religion.* Dr. Atkinson also contributed thirty articles to *Eerdmans Dictionary of the Bible,* and he has participated in several archaeological excavations in Israel and England.

ANN MARIE B. BAHR is professor of Religious Studies at South Dakota State University. Her areas of teaching, research, and writing include world religions, the New Testament, religion in American culture, and the Middle East. Her articles have appeared in *Annual Editions: World Religions 03/04* (McGraw-Hill, 2003), *The Journal of Ecumenical Studies,* and *Covenant for a New Creation: Ethics, Religion and Public Policy* (Orbis, 1991). Since 1999, she has authored a weekly newspaper column that analyzes the cultural significance of religious holidays. She has also served as president of the Upper Midwest Region of the American Academy of Religion.

MARTIN E. MARTY, an ordained minister in the Evangelical Lutheran Church in America, is the Fairfax M. Cone Distinguished Service Professor Emeritus at the University of Chicago Divinity School, where he taught for thirty-five years. Marty has served as president of the American Academy of Religion, the American Society of Church History, and the American Catholic Historical Association, and was also a member of two U.S. presidential commissions. He is currently Senior Regent at St. Olaf College in Northfield, Minnesota. Marty has written more than fifty books, including the three-volume *Modern American Religion* (University of Chicago Press). His book *Righteous Empire* was a recipient of the National Book Award.